# Dr. Anderson's Interpretive Guide to Old Testament Wisdom and Song (Job–Song of Songs)

By

STEVEN D. ANDERSON
Ph.D., Dallas Theological Seminary

**Dr. Anderson's Interpretive Guide to the Bible
Volume 3**

July 2015 edition

Cover photograph (taken by the author): cleft of a rock in Petra

Printed by CreateSpace, An Amazon.com Company

Self-published by the author

Author's webpage: http://Bible.TruthOnly.com
Author's blog: http://TruthOnlyBible.com

ISBN-10: 1500742996
ISBN-13: 978-1500742997

Citation for *The Chicago Manual of Style* (Turabian) and *The SBL Handbook of Style*:
Anderson, Steven D. *Dr. Anderson's Interpretive Guide to Old Testament Wisdom and Song (Job–Song of Songs)*. July 2015 ed. Dr. Anderson's Interpretive Guide to the Bible 3. Grand Rapids: Steven D. Anderson, 2015.

# Table of Contents

# Preface

The book you are reading is the third volume of an eight-volume series of interpretive guides for every book of the Bible. These interpretive guides originated in a massive, multi-year project that was part of my Ph.D. program in Biblical Studies at Dallas Theological Seminary, but they incorporate insights gained throughout a lifetime of Bible training and academic study.

All of the interpretive guides follow the same basic format and order: an introduction to the book; a discussion of introductory issues (such as author, date, writing style, and addressees); a paragraph-level subject outline of the book; an "argument" which traces the flow of thought throughout the book but also deals with macrostructure, theology, and interpretive issues; and an annotated bibliography. My bibliographies are not exhaustive, though some are more complete than others. My aim has been only to cite some important works. One does not need to read everything to arrive at the correct interpretation, and in fact cannot read everything if he tries.

These interpretive guides are similar enough to a Bible commentary so that some people would classify them as commentaries. However, they do not deal much with issues of translation or textual criticism, and do not deal extensively with interpretive details. This series is intended partly as an aid to reading, and partly as a starting point for more detailed exegesis. It is, essentially, a general guide to biblical interpretation, from which more specific interpretations may be developed. I believe that these guides fill a gap in the literature by providing a synthetic overview of every book of the Bible in a way that commentaries and introductions do not. Additionally, and more importantly, they are the product of my own careful study of the Scriptures, and are not simply a slightly revised repetition of what you can read in other resources.

My approach to the biblical text is also fairly unique for contemporary literature, which generally seeks to read the Bible through the grid of preformed theological ideas or background studies. My method of biblical interpretation emphasizes the primacy of the biblical text, and seeks to find its literal meaning. Although I use and often recommend recent commentaries and other scholarly literature, I am writing from a traditional point of view that you will not read in other contemporary literature.

My theological outlook is conservative and Baptistic. I believe in the inspiration and inerrancy of the Bible. I am opposed to destructive higher criticism, but not to scholarship. I am neither Calvinist nor Arminian. I hold to a premillennial, pretribulational eschatology; to a literal six-day creation; and to a literal and traditional interpretation of the Bible. There are few Bible scholars who agree on every detail of biblical interpretation and theology, but I think that most conservative evangelical students of the Bible will find these interpretive guides interesting and useful.

A word of warning on the bibliographies: there are many commentaries listed in my bibliographies for completeness or academic purposes which actually are bad, or even dangerous, works. It should not be assumed that a commentary is worth consulting simply because I have listed it in a bibliography. But scholars need to have a broad awareness of what other scholars are publishing.

Studying the Bible is a lifelong enterprise, and thus I plan to continually revise and update these interpretive guides as I continue to study God's Word. I welcome comments and specific corrections of typographical or grammatical errors, though I may not be able to respond to all feedback. See my author page at http://Bible.TruthOnly.com for contact information and information on electronic editions. My website also includes free downloads that are designed to accompany these interpretive guides, including Bible reading schedules, chronological charts, and a chart of David's mighty men. You can find my blog at http://TruthOnlyBible.com.

This book was originally published in August 2014. The July 2015 edition incorporates small editing changes and minor corrections supplied by readers.

Dr. Steven D. Anderson
Grand Rapids, Michigan

# Style Notes

*Quotations of the Bible*

Most extended biblical quotations in these interpretive guides are from the 1901 American Standard Version (ASV; not to be confused with the New American Standard Bible). Often the translation that I give is my own, or is my own modification of the ASV. Unlike more contemporary translations, the ASV is public domain, and can be quoted and modified freely without a publisher's permission or a royalty fee. I regard the ASV as the most accurate English Bible version, though I prefer to use the original Hebrew, Aramaic, or Greek text of the Bible.

*A Note on the Divine Name*

I usually use the divine name "Yahweh" (= "Jehovah") where it appears in the Hebrew text of the Old Testament, rather than substituting "the LORD." The fact that God the Father has a name has not historically been appreciated by the church, and still is not appreciated today, since the church has generally followed a Jewish superstition which developed during the intertestamental period by substituting "the LORD" for the personal name "Yahweh." While rendering יהוה as "the LORD" is theologically acceptable, it makes the Old Testament come alive when the reader realizes that Old Testament saints worshipped a God whose Person and name they knew, and did not merely know abstractly as "the LORD"—comparable in some ways to the use of "Jesus" as the personal name of God's Son in the New Testament. On the Jewish superstition which treats any utterance of the divine name as a sacrilege, see the following verses against it: Exod 3:15; 23:13; Josh 23:7; 1 Kgs 18:24-27, 36-37; Pss 20:7; 45:17; 69:36; Isa 56:6; Jer 44:26; Hos 2:17; Zech 13:2.

*Common Abbreviations*

For standard abbreviations used in the field of biblical studies, one can consult *The SBL Handbook of Style* (2nd ed.; Atlanta: SBL Press, 2014). Some common abbreviations used in these interpretive guides include:

ASV · · · · · · · · · · · 1901 American Standard Version
ch. · · · · · · · · · · · · · chapter
KJV · · · · · · · · · · · King James Version
LXX · · · · · · · · · · · Septuagint (an ancient Greek translation of the Old Testament)
MT · · · · · · · · · · · · Masoretic Text (the best preserved form of the Hebrew/Aramaic Old Testament)
NASB · · · · · · · · · New American Standard Bible
NIV · · · · · · · · · · · New International Version
NKJV · · · · · · · · · New King James Version
NRSV · · · · · · · · · New Revised Standard Version
NT · · · · · · · · · · · · New Testament
OT · · · · · · · · · · · · Old Testament
RSV · · · · · · · · · · · Revised Standard Version
v. · · · · · · · · · · · · · · verse
*v. l.* · · · · · · · · · · · · variant reading (*varia lectio*)

| | | | | |
|---|---|---|---|---|
| Gen | Genesis | Nah | Nahum |
| Exod | Exodus | Hab | Habakkuk |
| Lev | Leviticus | Zeph | Zephaniah |
| Num | Numbers | Hag | Haggai |
| Deut | Deuteronomy | Zech | Zechariah |
| Josh | Joshua | Mal | Malachi |
| Judg | Judges | Matt | Matthew |
| Ruth | Ruth | Mark | Mark |
| 1 Sam | 1 Samuel | Luke | Luke |
| 2 Sam | 2 Samuel | John | John |
| 1 Kgs | 1 Kings | Acts | Acts |
| 2 Kgs | 2 Kings | Rom | Romans |
| 1 Chr | 1 Chronicles | 1 Cor | 1 Corinthians |
| 2 Chr | 2 Chronicles | 2 Cor | 2 Corinthians |
| Ezra | Ezra | Gal | Galatians |
| Neh | Nehemiah | Eph | Ephesians |
| Esth | Esther | Phil | Philippians |
| Job | Job | Col | Colossians |
| Ps | Psalm | 1 Thess | 1 Thessalonians |
| Pss | Psalms | 2 Thess | 2 Thessalonians |
| Prov | Proverbs | 1 Tim | 1 Timothy |
| Eccl | Ecclesiastes | 2 Tim | 2 Timothy |
| Song | Song of Songs (Song of Solomon) | Tit | Titus |
| Isa | Isaiah | Phlm | Philemon |
| Jer | Jeremiah | Heb | Hebrews |
| Lam | Lamentations | James (or Jas) | James |
| Ezek | Ezekiel | 1 Pet | 1 Peter |
| Dan | Daniel | 2 Pet | 2 Peter |
| Hos | Hosea | 1 John | 1 John |
| Joel | Joel | 2 John | 2 John |
| Amos | Amos | 3 John | 3 John |
| Obad | Obadiah | Jude | Jude |
| Jonah (or Jon) | Jonah | Rev | Revelation |
| Mic | Micah | | |

# Interpretive Guide to Job

As a narrative record, Job is a historical book, and yet it is even more so a book of wisdom, since the point of the book is to teach practical theology, rather than to trace the development of history. For this reason, the body of the book consists of a record of speeches. The book of Job specifically addresses the issue of how to understand the suffering of righteous people in view of who God is. Job is the ideal paradigm of the innocent sufferer: he was the most righteous man in the entire world, perfect and blameless, yet suddenly everything he had was destroyed, including his wealth, his children, and, finally, his health, comfort, respectability, and friends. He seemed to have done nothing to deserve such a complete reversal of fortunes, and, when pressed, he wrongly vented his frustration on God. Job's suffering probably lasted no more than a few months, and the rest of his long life was quite pleasant and blessed—yet his suffering was so intense that he was brought in that short time almost as low as a man can go.

The book of Job is tremendously relevant, because undeserved suffering is endemic to the human experience. Virtually all Christians struggle to understand and endure the trials they face. We all tend to think when we suffer that we do not deserve it, and we have trouble figuring out why God will not answer our prayers to relieve our pain. Yet, oddly enough, most pastors would not even consider preaching through the entire book of Job—it is too long for them, and, frankly, they think the speeches are boring. They think it better to feed their flock the enervating pabulum of modern psychology and counseling theory. In reality, however, we need a book as long as Job in order to answer in detail the complex issues posed by undeserved suffering. Further, we need to hear God's answer to suffering, not man's answer. Far from being boring, the book of Job thoroughly addresses the questions we struggle with when we suffer. It does, however, take a considerable amount of study and reflection to really dig into the book and apprehend its wisdom.

Pastors need to prepare their people for suffering, because the Christian life is characterized by suffering. If we train people to think that God will cause things to go smoothly for us when we follow His will—which is what we naturally think we deserve anyway—then when things go awry, we start to question God's goodness and sovereignty. Alternatively, we think, "I must be doing something wrong. God would not let this happen to me if I was not." We need to think, "Suffering is a blessing which God gives to His own, just as prosperity is a blessing." Job 34:33 teaches that we have no right to refuse what God has given us (cf. 2:10). God knows what is best, and we cannot fully understand His ways. We must simply trust Him.

The book of Job is normally studied for the lessons it teaches about suffering, and rightly so. But this book is less a struggle to understand suffering than it is a struggle to understand God. The resolution only comes when Job finally sees who God is, which resolves all of his questions about suffering. Job repented of his complaint against God when He saw who God is, though he still lacked an explanation for his suffering, and still lay destitute and afflicted. We, too, should read this book with a view to seeing who God is, for our questions about suffering are ultimately questions about God, and they can only be resolved by coming to a proper understanding of God (cf. James 5:11).

## Author

The author of this book was probably Elihu. Only someone who had heard the speeches of chs. 3–41 could have written them down, which narrows the possible authors to Job, Eliphaz, Bildad, Zophar, and Elihu (postulating an unnamed bystander is too speculative).[1] Of these possible authors, Elihu would have been in the best position to write the work, since Job did not write the account of his death (42:16-17), without which the book would not have a fitting conclusion. Elihu was younger than Job and his friends (so 32:4-10), and therefore could have outlived Job. Whoever recorded the speeches obviously had a superb memory—as demonstrated by Elihu's frequent quotations of Job in his own speeches—and was supernaturally given perfect recollection by the Holy Spirit. He was also given by direct revelation the information concerning God's dialogues with Satan in heaven. The writer must have given the book to one of the Hebrew patriarchs, probably Abraham (see below under "Date"). Abraham may well have known Job when Job was in his later years, and could have confirmed the general outline of events from a variety of sources.[2] This book would then have been passed on to the elders of Israel through Isaac and Jacob. It is sometimes suggested that some changes were made to update the language of the book at some point—perhaps by Moses in the period between the Exodus (1446 B.C.) and the entrance into Canaan (1406 B.C.). However, the language of Job is unmistakably archaic, and the Canaanite language probably did not change so much from the time of Abraham to the time of Moses that a linguistic update would be required. There is no direct evidence for linguistic updating in the book.

The book of Job was written in Hebrew, which was the language of Canaan and many of the surrounding nations, such as Edom, Moab, and Ammon. However, there are some differences between the Hebrew of Job and the standard Classical Hebrew of the rest of the OT. The text of Job is difficult to read in Hebrew—the words and their usages are rare, and much of the grammar and syntax is irregular. This is probably due, in part, to the great age of the text, which therefore represents an unmodified earlier form of the language.

One peculiarity of the language of this book is the terminology it uses for God. The word אֵל, a relatively uncommon word for God in most books of the OT, occurs some fifty-five times in Job, and all of these are in the speeches.[3] The 236 uses of אֵל in the singular in the OT occur almost exclusively in the archaic language of Job and of the Pentateuch, and in the imitatively archaic language of the Psalter and Isaiah. Likewise, forty-one of the fifty-eight OT occurrences of אֱלוֹהַ are in Job, and all of these are in the speeches. Additionally, the book of Job contains thirty-one of the forty-eight OT occurrences of the term שַׁדַּי (*Almighty*), all of which are found in the speeches. On the other hand, אֱלֹהִים, the standard word for God in the other OT books, only occurs seventeen times in Job. Eleven of these occurrences are in the narrative of chs. 1–2, which was probably written 140 years after the speeches were uttered (i.e., after Job's death). Probably for the same reason, there is only one occurrence of the tetragrammaton (יהוה/*Yahweh*) in the main group of speeches, in 12:9, though this name occurs more regularly in the introduction (chs. 1–2) and conclusion (chs. 38–42).[4] Finally, the exceedingly common term אָדוֹן is used only twice in Job, and only once of God (with a *v. l.*).

Elihu was, in all probability, not a descendent of Abraham, and therefore was the only Gentile author of OT Scripture.

---

[1] The claim that Hebrew writing did not exist at this early period is based on an evolutionary view of history, and cannot be proved. It is not uncommon that a single archeological find will overturn masses of scholarly dogma.

[2] The suggestion that Abraham wrote the book himself, with the speeches dictated to him by Elihu, is not likely, since this would make Abraham nothing more than Elihu's scribe. Surely there were professional scribes available for the task, were Elihu not indeed able to write for himself.

[3] This does not count the use of אֵלִים in 41:25[17].

[4] Incidentally, the non-use of יהוה and אֱלֹהִים in the speeches, and the use of the other terms, shows that the speeches were not merely made up by the author, or even reconstructed in accordance with his recollections, but were recorded with precise historical accuracy.

## Date, Setting, and Occasion of Writing

The book of Job is not dated by any specific chronological markers, but enough is said to determine that it was written at about the time of Abraham, i.e., around 2200–2100 B.C., about 300 years after the flood. It is clear from the descriptions of behemoth and leviathan in chs. 40–41 that large dinosaurs were still fairly common in Job's day—a characteristic of the early postdiluvian period. The existence of distinct nations in the book of Job shows that Job lived at least after the division of the nations at Babel. Job's wealth, like that of the patriarchs, was primarily measured by livestock rather than precious metals (1:3; 42:12). Job's lifespan is also like that of the patriarchs—he already has ten adult children when the story begins, then lives 140 years afterward. Job definitely did not live after the giving of the Law at Sinai, since he acted as a priest on behalf of his family (1:5), and kept camels (1:17), which were unclean under the Law (Lev 11:4). Since at the start of his troubles Job was called the most righteous man on earth (1:8; 2:3), it is likely that the earlier period of Job's life occurred when Abraham was a young man, or even before Abraham was born. In any case, it is still interesting that God chose Abraham rather than Job as the progenitor of the Messiah's people. Job obviously had contact with one or more of the Israelite patriarchs, or else this story would not have been transmitted as part of the Hebrew Scriptures. Probably Abraham came to Canaan toward the end of Job's life, though he may have already heard of his story.

It would appear that Job not only lived at about the time of Abraham (or slightly earlier), but also in about the same area as Abraham, i.e., near the land of Canaan. Job is said to be one of "the sons of the east" (1:3), a term which is almost always applied in the Bible to the peoples who lived in the semiarid land east and southeast of Canaan.[5] That Job lived near Canaan is confirmed by the reference to the flood of the Jordan River in 40:23. Had Job lived near Egypt, the Nile flood would have been referenced, while the Tigris or Euphrates would have been referenced had he lived near Mesopotamia. The "jungle of the Jordan" also seems like a more suitable biome for giant dinosaurs after the flood than the plains of Mesopotamia or Egypt. According to 6:16, Job lived in a climate where he saw snow and ice, which occurs in the highlands east of the Jordan, but not in Egypt or Babylonia.

The other places and peoples mentioned in the book of Job appear to confirm the location of Job east/southeast of Canaan. Job is said to have lived in the land of Uz (1:1), which must have been named after a son of Aram (Gen 10:23). Lamentations 4:21 specifically identifies its location as including the territory of Edom. The oldest of Job's friends, Eliphaz, is called "the Temanite," meaning that he lived in or near Teman. The word תֵּימָן means "south" (like נֶגֶב), but was also a standard reference for a region in what became Edomite territory. Tema (תֵּמָא), an oasis in northern Saudi Arabia where the Neo-Babylonian monarch Nabonidus famously spent ten years, is mentioned in 6:19. The same verse mentions Sheba (שְׁבָא), which in Hebrew is exactly the same term as "Sabeans" (שְׁבָא) in 1:15—the people which made a raid on Job's livestock. Sheba was a people and a kingdom in southern Arabia which evidently also maintained trading colonies in northern Arabia. Another group which made a raid on Job's livestock was the Chaldeans (1:17); they were an Aramaic-speaking tribe located in Babylonia later in biblical history, but were nomadic in earlier periods. Job's friend Bildad is called "the Shuhite" (הַשּׁוּחִי), i.e., someone from the city/region/tribe of Shuah (שׁוּחַ). The only "Shuah" named in the Bible is a son of Abraham by Keturah (Gen 25:2), which confirms the antiquity of the name but does not reveal anything about the Shuah with which Bildad was associated. Job's friend Zophar is called "the Naamathite" (הַנַּעֲמָתִי), i.e., someone from the city/region/tribe of Naamah (נַעֲמָה), an unknown location. Elihu, as the writer of the book, gives the most complete information about himself: "the son of Barachel the Buzite, of

---

[5] It is so used in Judg 6:3, 33; 7:12; 8:10; 1 Kgs 4:30; Isa 11:14; Jer 49:28; Ezek 25:4, 10. The lone exception is Gen 29:1, where it is used to refer to Paddan-aram.

the family of Ram." Of these three identifiers, the most helpful one is "the Buzite," meaning that Elihu was from a location called "Buz." Buz is associated in Jer 25:23 with the Arab desert tribes of Dedan and Tema.[6] The topaz of Cush is noted in 28:19; it certainly was traded in and around Canaan, but would not have been as well known in the more distant Mesopotamia. Finally, the gold of Ophir is noted in 22:24 and 28:16. The location of Ophir is disputed, though Solomon brought gold from Ophir through the port of Ezion-geber in Edom (2 Chr 8:17-18).

In summary, all of the geographical indicators given in the book of Job point to a geographical setting east/southeast of the land of Canaan, probably in what was later known as the land of Edom. The chronological indicators in the book of Job point to the events of the body of the book occurring before the call of Abraham, but with Job's death occurring after Abraham's arrival in Canaan. If Job lived about 225 years, he may have been born around 2275 (243 years after the Flood), the main events of the book may have occurred around 2200 (44 years before the birth of Abraham), and Job may have died around 2050 (shortly after the birth of Isaac in 2066). Elihu must have written the book around 2050, possibly in conjunction with Abraham. This easily makes Job the oldest book in the canon, predating the Pentateuch by about 650 years. There is no more appropriate subject for the earliest book in the canon than an investigation into the nature of God, and how man is to relate to his Creator.[7]

## Purpose and Message

The purpose of the book of Job is to provide a theological framework for understanding the undeserved suffering of righteous people in view of God's sovereignty and moral perfection. The message of the book of Job is that God, and God alone, is competent to rule the world. Man is in no position to question God's wisdom or to demand that God give an account of Himself. Since man is not in a position of omniscience, he often will not understand why God does what He does, but should nevertheless trust that His governance of the universe and His treatment of individuals is just and good, and will turn out for the good of the righteous in the end.

## Outline of Job

*Summary Outline*

I. Initial Setting and Events 1:1–2:13
II. Speeches of Job and His Friends 3:1–31:40
III. Elihu's Speech 32:1–37:24
IV. God's Speeches 38:1–41:34
V. Job's Repentance and Restoration 42:1-17

---

[6] The name "Barachel" does not appear elsewhere in Scripture, and so is not helpful as an identifier. The suggestion that Elihu was an Israelite from the family of Ram the son of Hezron, the son of Perez, the son of Judah is impossible. Ram is never given as a family name elsewhere on the Old Testament, and it seems that the events of the book of Job occurred well before Ram's birth. There are at least two other people named Ram in the Old Testament, so it was probably a fairly common Semitic name.

[7] In its themes and language, Job can justly be compared to Isaiah 40–48, another theodicy.

*Expanded Outline*

**I. Initial Setting and Events 1:1–2:13**
   A. Job's initial situation 1:1-5
   B. The first round of affliction 1:6-22
      1. God's first challenge to Satan 1:6-12
      2. The destruction of Job's possessions 1:13-19
      3. Job's response 1:20-22
   C. The second round of affliction 2:1-13
      1. God's second challenge to Satan 2:1-6
      2. Job smitten 2:7-10
      3. The visit of Job's friends 2:11-13

**II. Speeches of Job and His Friends 3:1–31:40**
   A. Job's first speech 3:1-26
      1. The wish not to have been born 3:1-19
      2. The prayer for death 3:20-26
   B. Eliphaz's first speech 4:1–5:27
      1. Eliphaz's accusation 4:1-11
      2. Eliphaz's dream 4:12-21
      3. The insecurity of the wicked 5:1-7
      4. Call to repent 5:8-16
      5. The restoration to follow repentance 5:17-26
      6. Conclusion 5:27
   C. Job's second speech 6:1–7:21
      1. Job's wretchedness 6:1-7
      2. Job's request for death 6:8-13
      3. Job's complaint about his friends' treachery 6:14-23
      4. Job's reproof of his friends' false accusation 6:24-30
      5. Job's complaint regarding the wearisomeness and transitoriness of his life 7:1-10
      6. Job remonstrates with God 7:11-21
   D. Bildad's first speech 8:1-22
      1. Bildad's affirmation of prosperity theology and its application to Job 8:1-7
      2. Appeal to history 8:8-10
      3. The insecurity of the wicked 8:11-19
      4. Job's hope of restoration 8:20-22
   E. Job's third speech 9:1–10:22
      1. Job's helplessness before God 9:1-12
      2. The accusation of divine injustice 9:13-24
      3. The unprofitability of righteousness claimed 9:25-35
      4. The charge of wrongdoing 10:1-7
      5. Job's protest of God's treatment of him 10:8-17
      6. The request for a peaceful end 10:18-22
   F. Zophar's first speech 11:1-20
      1. Zophar's contradiction of Job 11:1-6
      2. God's knowledge of Job's hypocrisy 11:7-12
      3. Counsel to repent in order to be restored 11:13-20
   G. Job's fourth speech 12:1–14:22
      1. Job's argument against his friends 12:1–13:2
         a. Job's contradiction of his friends 12:1-6
         b. The universal recognition of the falsity of his friends' claim 12:7-12
         c. God as the sole source of wisdom 12:13-25

            d. Job's understanding of wisdom 13:1-2
        2. Job's argument against God 13:3-28
            a. Job's rejection of his friends' judgment 13:3-12
            b. Job's assertion of his righteousness 13:13-19
            c. Job's demand that God cease afflicting him 13:20-28
        3. Job's complaint to God 14:1-22
            a. Job's plea from man's frailty 14:1-6
            b. Job's plea from man's mortality 14:7-12
            c. Job's plea for a respite from life 14:13-17
            d. Job's complaint over man's lot 14:18-22
H. Eliphaz's second speech 15:1-35
    1. Eliphaz's condemnation of Job's speech 15:1-6
    2. Eliphaz's rebuke of Job's presumptuousness 15:7-16
    3. The speedy destruction of the wicked 15:17-35
I. Job's fifth speech 16:1–17:16
    1. Job's rebuke of his friends 16:1-5
    2. Job's complaint over God's treatment of him 16:6-17
    3. The call for witnesses to the injustice of Job's death 16:18-22
    4. The call for a heavenly Witness against Job's friends 17:1-5
    5. Job's accusation against his friends 17:6-16
J. Bildad's second speech 18:1-21
    1. Bildad's rebuke of Job's speeches 18:1-4
    2. The misfortunes of the wicked man 18:5-21
K. Job's sixth speech 19:1-29
    1. Job's rebuke of his friends' harshness 19:1-6
    2. Job's complaint of divine injustice 19:7-12
    3. Job's appeal for pity in light of his social estrangement 19:13-22
    4. Job's anticipation of vindication 19:23-29
L. Zophar's second speech 20:1-29
    1. The swift end of the wicked 20:1-11
    2. The total bereavement of the wicked 20:12-19
    3. The portion of the wicked man 20:20-29
M. Job's seventh speech 21:1-34
    1. The appeal to keep silent 21:1-6
    2. The prosperity of the wicked 21:7-16
    3. The end of the wicked 21:17-26
    4. The end of all men 21:27-34
N. Eliphaz's third speech 22:1-30
    1. Eliphaz's accusations against Job 22:1-11
    2. God's knowledge of Job's sins 22:12-20
    3. Exhortation to repentance for restoration 22:21-30
O. Job's eighth speech 23:1–24:25
    1. Job's wish for access to God 23:1-9
    2. Job's integrity in his trials 23:10-17
    3. God's indifference to oppression 24:1-12
    4. The fate of the rebel 24:13-21
    5. The fate of the righteous 24:22-25
P. Bildad's third speech 25:1-6
Q. Job's ninth speech 26:1–31:40
    1. Introduction 26:1-14
        a. Job's rebuke of Bildad 26:1-4

b. God's power and majesty affirmed 26:5-14
2. Job's instruction of his friends 27:1–28:28
 a. Job's knowledge of God's dealings with the wicked 27:1-23
  i. Job's asseveration of his righteousness and prayer for vengeance 27:1-12
  ii. The vanity of the hope of the godless 27:13-23
 b. Job's wisdom parable 28:1-28
  i. Man's skill in bringing treasure out of earth's depths 28:1-11
  ii. Wisdom more difficult to obtain 28:12-22
  iii. Wisdom obtainable only from God 28:23-28
3. Job's reflection on his personal state 29:1–31:40
 a. Job's recollection of the happiness of his former state 29:1-25
 b. Job bemoans his present affliction 30:1-31
  i. Job's derision from society's dregs 30:1-15
  ii. Job's present affliction under the hand of God 30:16-23
  iii. Job bewails the injustice and wretchedness of his condition 30:24-31
 c. Job's asseveration of his integrity 31:1-40
  i. What Job believes he deserves from God 31:1-4
  ii. Job's truthful character 31:5-8
  iii. Job's faithfulness to his wife 31:9-12
  iv. Job's justice to his workers 31:13-15
  v. Job's assistance to vulnerable people 31:16-23
  vi. Job's rejection of idolatry 31:24-28
  vii. Job's purity of heart 31:29-36
  viii. Job's fair business practices 31:37-40a
  ix. Job rests his case 31:40b

**III. Elihu's Speech 32:1–37:24**
A. Introductory 32:1-22
 1. Elihu provoked to wrath 32:1-5
 2. Elihu's reason for waiting 32:6-10
 3. Elihu's rebuke of Job's friends 32:11-14
 4. Elihu's thoughts to himself 32:15-22
B. Elihu's defense of God's dealings with man 33:1-33
 1. Elihu's appeal to Job 33:1-7
 2. Elihu's identification of Job's error 33:8-12
 3. God's communication through visions 33:13-18
 4. God's communication through chastisement 33:19-22
 5. God's communication through intermediaries 33:23-28
 6. Elihu's challenge to Job 33:29-33
C. Elihu's vindication of God's justice 34:1-37
 1. Elihu's rebuke of Job's claim of divine injustice 34:1-9
 2. The impossibility of the Creator and Sustainer of man to sin 34:10-15
 3. The impossibility of the Governor of the world to sin 34:16-20
 4. Elihu's defense of God's treatment of the wicked 34:21-30
 5. Elihu's rebuke of Job's rebellion against God's sovereignty 34:31-37
D. Elihu's defense of God's sovereignty 35:1-16
 1. God's judicial passivity 35:1-8
 2. God's rejection of impious prayers 35:9-16
E. Elihu's defense of God's use of affliction 36:1-23
 1. God's purposes in bringing affliction 36:1-16
 2. Call to Job to accept his affliction 36:17-23
F. Call to humble oneself before the sovereign God 36:24–37:24

1. Call to magnify God for His awesome majesty 36:24-33
2. God's sovereignty displayed in the winter storm 37:1-13
3. The absolute impossibility of instructing God 37:14-20
4. Summary of the argument and announcement of God's arrival 37:21-24

**IV. God's Speeches 38:1–41:34**
   A. God's first speech 38:1–40:2
      1. Introduction 38:1-3
      2. God's sovereignty over and knowledge of non-living things 38:1-38
         a. God's creation of the earth 38:4-7
         b. God's creation and governance of the sea 38:8-11
         c. God's creation and governance of the light 38:12-15
         d. God's knowledge of the unsearchable 38:16-18
         e. God's knowledge of natural forces 38:19-24
         f. God's knowledge and governance of precipitation 38:25-30
         g. God's knowledge and governance of the celestial world 38:31-33
         h. God's governance of storms 38:34-38
      3. God's sovereignty over and knowledge of living things 38:39–39:30
         a. God's provision of prey for young lions and ravens—helpless animals 38:39-41
         b. God's knowledge of the wild goats—distant animals 39:1-4
         c. God's sovereignty over the wild ass and the wild ox—untamable animals 39:5-12
         d. God's creation of the ostrich—a stupid but strong animal 39:13-18
         e. God's creation of the horse—a steely animal 39:19-25
         f. God's creation of the hawk and the eagle—high flying animals 39:26-30
      4. God's demand for an answer 40:1-2
   B. Job's first response 40:3-5
   C. God's second speech 40:6–41:34
      1. Renewal of God's challenge to Job 40:6-14
      2. God's creation of behemoth—the strongest animal 40:15-24
      3. God's creation of leviathan—the fiercest animal 41:1-34
         a. God's power demonstrated by leviathan's power 41:1-11
         b. Description of leviathan 41:12-34

**V. Job's Repentance and Restoration 42:1-17**
   A. Job's repentance 42:1-6
   B. The repentance of Job's friends 42:7-9
   C. Job's prosperity restored 42:10-17

### Argument of Job

The overall structure of the book of Job is fairly straightforward: the initial setting and events (chs. 1-2), the speeches of Job and his friends (chs. 3–31), Elihu's speech (chs. 32–37), God's speeches (chs. 38–41), and Job's repentance and restoration (ch. 42). Between three chapters of narrative are thirty-nine chapters of dialogues, with limited narrative in the dialogues. The focus of the book is thus obviously on the dialogues, in which the nature of God and His dealings with man are discussed. Before going through the book paragraph by paragraph, an overview of the argument will be presented.

Job and his friends began with a wrong theology, a theology which said that personal righteousness must result in physical prosperity, because a just and sovereign God will give people what they deserve. When Job suddenly had an experience that contradicted his theology, he began to question God. He knows that he is righteous, yet suffering immensely, and he also suddenly becomes aware of the prosperity of the unrighteous about him. Job complains that this is not fair—he is not getting what he deserves, and they are not getting what they deserve. There is simply no good cause, in his mind, for what has happened to him. If God is just and sovereign, how can He allow this? Job senses that God will do what is right and vindicate him in the end, but he thinks that God's treatment of him is simply unjustifiable. Job does not know how to revise his theology or make sense of it all. He seems to alternate in his speeches between saying "God is unjust for doing this to me," and "I will trust in God until I die, and rely on him for my help." But he finds that the two attitudes cannot produce a coherent theology. Job finally settles on the assertion that he is more righteous than God; and although he does not renounce his faith in God or his loyalty to God, he does demand a hearing with God so he can present his case. Readers tend to sympathize with Job, who is far more undeserving of suffering than they are and has suffered as much as he can without dying—yet they feel that somewhere he has gone wrong in his attempt to understand his ordeal.

Job's three friends exemplify the common thinking, which equates righteousness with physical blessing and unrighteousness with physical affliction and does not recognize exceptions. The reader knows this thinking to be wrong, at least in its application to Job, because of the introduction which affirms Job's righteousness and explains that Job's suffering was not a result of his sin. As Job's friends continually accuse him of wrongdoing—without proof—and implore him to repent in order to be healed, the reader is supposed to keep thinking, "That is exactly what I would have said, but it is wrong." If there was ever a clear-cut case where a man's suffering was undoubtedly coming from God as direct divine chastisement, it would seem to have been Job's. When Job loses everything at once—including by fire falling from heaven and consuming his sheep—it is clearly neither a coincidence nor a natural occurrence. When he is then smitten with the most miserable type of illness imaginable, it seems unmistakable that God is smiting him. In a sense it *was* true that God was smiting Job (so 2:3), though He was not doing so directly—He had allowed Satan to do so. What was not true was the proposition that the only reason a righteous and just God could smite people is in retribution for their sin. In fact, at a later point in history God would give His own Son over to the most cruel and undeserved death ever suffered, yet without violating His perfect justice—and Jesus accepted His suffering because it was part of God's plan.

After Job and his three friends conclude their speeches in bitter disagreement, two new participants are introduced—Elihu and God. Elihu, a young bystander, represents the viewpoint of a man with the right theology, and the right application of theology to Job's experience. As Elihu argues God's case, Job has no response because he realizes Elihu is right. Finally, God Himself appears to pick up the argument where Elihu left it off. When God at last speaks, He does not tell Job why He did what He did; He only asks a series of questions to prove His might and wisdom. The introduction tells the reader what prompted Job's trials, but Job does not need to know the reason to reach a resolution.[8] The lesson for us is that we do not need to know all the reasons why things happen, either; we can rest confidently in the wisdom of God as He rules the universe. Further, it is abundantly clear that both Job and all readers of his book are better off for his trials, that God did in fact have a good reason to allow Job's suffering, and that He did actually treat Job with extreme graciousness in the end (cf. James 5:11).

---

[8] The resolution of the book of Job, like the resolution of the book of Habakkuk, is totally unlike any other theodicy of the ancient Near East. In "The Poem of the Righteous Sufferer" (in *CoS* 1:483-95), which has disingenuously been compared to Job, the suppliant only considers Marduk worthy to be praised because he has healed the sufferer. Job concludes that Yahweh is worthy to be praised because He is inherently worthy to be praised, and he comes to this conclusion before he is healed. Many of the biblical laments are composed prior to restoration, and praise Yahweh in anticipation of restoration. They are designed to help people who pray who have not yet reached a resolution. The inherent worthiness of Yahweh is affirmed simply by the fact that one comes to Him with his lament. There are also other significant differences between Mesopotamian "theodicies" and biblical ones: there is no concept in Mesopotamia of a personal relationship between the gods and the people, and so no resolution through meeting the person of the gods; there is no concept of the gods always doing what is right and wise and logical; and the gods fight with each other for control of the world, with none having total sovereignty.

## *Initial Setting and Events, 1:1–2:13*

The first two chapters of Job give the historical background for the theological argumentation which comprises the bulk of the book.

*Job's initial situation, 1:1-5.* The book of Job opens with a description of Job's initial situation, before his troubles began. He was perfect and upright, and he had the greatest wealth of anyone in his region. Detailed information is given about his children to explain what happens to them next.

*The first round of affliction, 1:6-22.* The first round of Job's affliction is described in 1:6-22. In this episode, Job loses everything but his health (and his unhelpful wife), yet takes it in stride. The affliction is initiated by God, who brags about Job to Satan (1:6-8).[9] After Satan falsely accuses Job, God allows Satan to test Job by afflicting him, within divinely ordained limits which Satan is bound to keep (1:9-12). Satan proceeds to destroy all of Job's possessions and to kill all of his servants and children, except for four servants who escaped alone to bring Job the bad news (1:13-19). Job's incredible response was exactly the opposite of what Satan had confidently predicted—Satan claimed that Job only blessed God because God blessed him, yet when God's blessing was taken away, Job blessed God anyway (1:20-22). Job did not worship God because of what God gave him, but because of who God is. Job also proved that even though he had great riches, his contentment never did stem from his possessions. Satan was clearly the loser in this battle.

*The second round of affliction, 2:1-13.* Chapter 2 tells the story of Job's second round of affliction. It begins with another boast by God to Satan concerning Job, and another false accusation by Satan which leads to God permitting Satan to afflict Job's person (2:1-6). The next paragraph describes the result: Satan smote Job with the most agonizing non-fatal chronic condition imaginable, yet when his wife speaks as Satan's mouthpiece to move Job to renounce his allegiance to God, he refuses to do so (2:7-10). When Job's three friends, Eliphaz, Bildad, and Zophar, come to Job to comfort him, they sit with him for seven days and nights to go through his trial with him (2:11-13). The scene is now set for the speeches to begin.

## *Speeches of Job and His Friends, 3:1–31:40*

The largest section of the book of Job, chs. 3–31, records the speeches of Job and his three friends. One must take care when quoting verses from these speeches, for false opinions are often expressed in them. However, all four of these men were believers, and they also say much that is true. Job, in particular, says much truth in his speeches. Even though Job's attitude is wrong, the fact that he was more righteous than his friends means that he says more things that are right and wise and memorable than they. The book of Job as a whole teaches truth rather than error, though it accomplishes this aim, in part, by quoting common but erroneous opinions. A key to determining to the truth content of statements in the speeches, as well as to interpreting the book as a whole, is to follow the argument of each speaker. The argument being made will, in turn, help one determine the accuracy of the statements made.[10]

---

[9] Liberal commentators, who hold to prosperity theology in rejection of the message of the book, cannot understand the justice in God's challenge to Satan. In reality, it is for some reason necessary for God to brag about believers in response to Satan's accusations, and to prove to Satan that his charges are false. In addition, God knew that in the end Satan's challenge would be good for Job and good for every believer who heard Job's story. Job's testing revealed hidden character flaws that he otherwise would never have realized existed, and Job became a better person by dealing with them.

*Job's first speech, 3:1-26.* After seven days of sitting quietly with his friends, Job finally breaks the silence with a bitter curse against the day of his own birth (3:1-19). After wishing that that he had never been born, Job prays for a speedy death to terminate the life which he so loathes (3:20-26).

*Eliphaz's first speech, 4:1–5:27.* Eliphaz was apparently the eldest and best respected of Job's friends, so he spoke first, and spoke the most. He clearly is a believer, and some of what he says is true—Job 5:13 is quoted by Paul in 1 Cor 3:19—but the main thrust of what he says is theologically erroneous (so 42:7). In 4:1-11, Eliphaz states the basic thesis for which he and his three friends will proceed to argue in the remainder of the dialogue: righteousness always brings blessing, and wickedness always brings trouble; therefore, Job's trouble is a result of sins that he has committed in secret. God is trying to get Job's attention in order to move him to repentance. Eliphaz begins his speech ominously, by rebuking Job for his anticipated negative reaction to it (4:2)—a sure indication of misguided counsel. In 4:12-21, Eliphaz presents a dream that he had as divine confirmation of his accusation. However, since this dream contains suspect theology, and Eliphaz only saw a vague form, this may have been nothing more than a normal, naturally occurring dream, not a supernatural revelation. Regardless, it shows the danger of putting one's faith in visions instead of in God's Word (or publicly revealed truth, at that early point in history).

After presenting his thesis and its "proof," Eliphaz warns Job of the insecurity and ultimate destruction which befalls the unrepentant (5:1-7), and calls upon him to repent (5:8-16). Eliphaz then describes the restoration of prosperity which will follow Job's repentance (5:17-26), and affirms that this is the analysis and course of action that the three friends have agreed is the right one (5:27); Eliphaz has represented the opinion of the entire group. Eliphaz ends his speech the same way he began it, which is by asserting that his counsel is for Job's good, as a foolish protest against the grief that he sensed it would cause (5:27).

*Job's second speech, 6:1–7:21.* Job clearly was injured rather than improved by his friend's accusatory speech, and he responds bitterly in chs. 6–7. Job begins his second speech by complaining about his wretched state (6:1-7). He then calls upon God to slay him in order to end his misery (6:8-13). In 6:14-23, Job begins to speak about his three friends, using the plural "you" as he complains about their treachery. [11] In 6:24-30 he addresses them directly, reproving them for falsely accusing him of unrighteousness. In ch. 7, Job shifts from a response to his friends for their poor advice to a response to God for placing him in such a miserable condition. In 7:1-10, Job complains about the wearisomeness (7:1-5) and transitoriness (7:6-10) of his life. He then addresses God directly, and for the first time lashes out at God for causing him such suffering (7:11-21). Job says many things in this final paragraph that he would later regret, and essentially accuses God of wrongdoing.

*Bildad's first speech, 8:1-22.* Bildad, who was likely the second-eldest of Job's friends, speaks next. Bildad should have affirmed that God's ways are inscrutable and Job has no right to question them, no right to claim that it is wrong for God to allow the righteous to suffer. Instead, Bildad does exactly the opposite, openly affirming the prosperity theology of the group (8:1-7): God is just, and gives men what they deserve; therefore, the suffering of Job and his children shows they are not righteous. If Job repents, God will restore his prosperity. In 8:8-10, Bildad appeals to history as proof of prosperity theology. He

---

[10] Also, one can refer to Elihu's speeches for remarks that are specifically criticized. Checking cross references, such as those indexed in NA[28] and *The Treasury of Scripture Knowledge* (TSK), can also be helpful for determining which statements are good or bad.

[11] One key to understanding Job's speeches is that most 3ms ("he") and 2ms ("thou") references in his speeches are to God, while the 2mp ("ye") references are to his three friends.

then describes how the wicked are insecure and will come to ruin (8:11-19), and pictures how Job will be restored when he repents (8:20-22).

*Job's third speech, 9:1–10:22.* Once again, Job's friends had hurt him rather than helping him, pushing him over the edge of desperation. In response to his friends' unfounded accusations and prosperity theology, Job becomes increasingly insistent upon his own uprightness, and also becomes increasingly settled upon the idea that God is treating him unjustly. Chapters 9–10 are one of the low points in Job's speeches. Although this speech is a reaction to Bildad's, Job is really responding to God in these chapters. He does so in bitterness and anger, repeatedly accusing God of wrongdoing. It is important to note, however, that Job's faith in God never wavers, nor does he renounce his loyalty to God, or doubt God's Word or His historic acts. Job begins in 9:1-12 by bemoaning his helplessness in the face of God's infinite power. In 9:13-24, Job lets loose on God, affirming that God has no right to cause him to suffer, and complaining that God destroys the perfect and the wicked together. In 9:25-35, Job wrongly affirms that there is no profit in righteousness (cf. 35:3), and demands an impartial umpire to judge between himself and God—implying that the umpire would find God guilty of doing wrong, and would justify Job. Job directly charges God with wrongdoing in 10:1-7, saying that God has abused His power and is treating Job as if he is wicked, even though he is not wicked. Job continues to protest God's treatment of him in 10:8-17, affirming that there is no good reason for what God is doing to him. In 10:14, Job wrongly asserts, on the basis of prosperity theology, that God has refused to forgive his sin. The speech concludes in 10:18-22 with Job requesting a peaceful end to his short and vain life.

*Zophar's first speech, 11:1-20.* Zophar, the youngest of Job's three friends, responds to Job's speech by directly contradicting him: God is fully justified in causing Job to suffer, and in fact is punishing Job less than his sins deserve (11:1-6). Of course, Zophar does not have any direct evidence for such sins, and is simply continuing the false assumption that God does not allow the righteous to suffer. Zophar then appeals to God's unsearchableness and omniscience as evidence that Job has committed some secret sins that no one else knows about, and that God is bringing these to remembrance (11:7-12). Zophar proceeds to repeat the advice of Job's first two friends: Job must repent of his sins, and when he does so, his troubles will go away (11:13-20). The trio of friends cannot come up with any other answer to Job's suffering, because they cannot imagine that suffering would be part of God's plan for the righteous. Each speech simply repeats the same tired, worn out prosperity theology.

*Job's fourth speech, 12:1–14:22.* Job responds to Zophar by directly contradicting him, asserting that they are fools, Job himself is righteous, and in fact the righteous do suffer and the wicked do prosper (12:1-6). The claim of Job's friends that they knew more than he because wisdom resides in the elderly is false (12:7-12; cf. 15:10; 32:6-9)—in fact, wisdom resides in God, who confounds the counsel of elders and princes (12:13-25); therefore Job, who knows all this, is not inferior to his friends in wisdom (13:1-2). Job then dismisses his friends' speeches, saying that they are worthless words and present false claims about God; Job really is speaking to God, not to his unreasonable friends (13:3-12). Then Job, like his friends, returns to his old refrain, asserting his own righteousness before God, and implying that he is actually more righteous than God (13:13-19). He then addresses God instead of his friends, accusing God of injustice and demanding that God cease from afflicting him (13:20-28). He argues that because man is frail and helpless, God should leave him alone instead of pressing upon him (14:1-6); if he brings a man to an early death, he will not live again until the resurrection which follows the destruction of the present creation (14:7-12). Yet Job would rather die and wait in the grave for resurrection than live without a respite from God's wrath (14:13-17). Job then complains over man's lot, since every man's hope of life is eventually crushed in death, and in the interim his mind and body are racked with pain (14:18-22).

*Eliphaz's second speech, 15:1-35.* Since all three of Job's friends have already spoken, they now commence a second round of speeches, beginning once again with Eliphaz, who, predictably, was unmoved by Job's arguments, and responds by strongly assaulting Job. He condemns Job's speech, and repeats the accusation that Job is full of iniquity (15:1-6). He arrogantly belittles Job for thinking that he is wiser than they are, and rebukes him for his presumptuousness against both his friends and God (15:7-16). After attacking Job, Eliphaz returns to the same tired answer: good deeds bring good times, evil deeds bring hard times, therefore Job's suffering is a punishment for his sin (15:17-35).

*Job's fifth speech, 16:1–17:16.* Job begins his fifth speech by condemning his friends for their failure to comfort him, imploring them to keep silent (16:1-5). Job then returns to the same old complaint over God's treatment of him, railing against God for afflicting him, while asserting that he himself is pure (i.e., and God is not; 16:6-17). In 16:18-22, Job calls both the earth and a heavenly Intercessor (the Son of God?) to witness the justice of his cause and the injustice of his death. He then calls for his divine Intercessor to witness against the treachery of his friends and take vengeance upon them (17:1-5). Job then addresses his friends directly in 17:6-16, accusing them of being unrighteous and unwise, unable to prove their claim that he is wicked, and holding out a false hope of restoration.

*Bildad's second speech, 18:1-21.* The responses of Job's friends continue in order, with Bildad answering next. He rebukes Job for his speech and for his condemnation of his friends, and says Job's angry words are empty and ineffective; he sarcastically asks whether the earth will tear itself in response to Job's hollow call to it (18:1-4). After this crass display of insensitivity, Bildad quickly returns to the same old answer—the wicked always suffer, and the righteous are always blessed. Bildad's description of the misfortunes of the wicked man in 18:5-21 is a thinly veiled description of Job's misfortunes, and his conclusion in 18:21—"Surely such are the dwellings of the unrighteous, and this is the place of him that knoweth not God"—is meant to apply to Job.

*Job's sixth speech, 19:1-29.* As the circular dialogue continues, Job rebukes his friends for their harsh words toward one who is suffering under the hand of God (19:1-6). He then complains once again about God's unjust treatment of him, using words that Elihu would later rebuke him for (19:7-12; cf. 33:10). Job then bemoans his social estrangement, and appeals to his friends to just have pity on him instead of persecuting him (19:13-22). He finally cries out for vindication (19:23-24), anticipating total restoration in the resurrection (19:25-27), and anticipating temporal vengeance upon his treacherous friends (19:28-29).

*Zophar's second speech, 20:1-29.* Zophar, who is third in the order of Job's friends, now speaks again. He does not deride Job directly, but repeats the same theology that the three friends have been propounding all along. Zophar describes the misfortunes suffered by the wicked man—his swift end (20:1-11), his total loss of everything (20:12-19), and his portion from God (20:20-29). The implication, once again, is that Job must be wicked, since this is Job's portion.

*Job's seventh speech, 21:1-34.* In Job's seventh speech, he finally responds to his friends' claim that the wicked always come to destruction and do not prosper. Job begins, once again, by appealing to his friends to keep silence (21:1-6). Job's response to his friends' claim that suffering is a penalty for sin is that experience does not bear this out: the wicked often do prosper in this life, and die in peace (21:7-16). However, the wicked are all brought to the grave eventually, whether after a life of ease or a life of sorrow (21:17-26). In fact, all men are brought to the grave, whether righteous or wicked, whether prosperous or poor, to be recompensed at the final day of judgment (21:27-34). This is one of Job's better speeches; he is correct to observe that the wicked often prosper, and is also correct to observe the reason: God is waiting to recompense them until the ultimate day of judgment. He does not, however, transfer these observations to his own experience.

*Eliphaz's third speech, 22:1-30.* Although Job has now put the lie to his friends' prosperity theology, they are not convinced. Instead, in Eliphaz's third and final speech, he gives the strongest and most condemnatory statement yet of prosperity theology and its application to Job. In 22:1-11, Eliphaz finally states directly what has been implied all along: Job's trouble is punishment for his sins. He makes up a series of false charges against Job in 22:5-9, which are really unsubstantiated guesses at Job's secret sins. In 22:12-20, he affirms God's knowledge of Job's sins, and offers Job's suffering as proof that God is paying Job back for his wickedness. In 22:21-30, Eliphaz promises Job restoration and an easy life if only he will repent.

*Job's eighth speech, 23:1–24:25.* In his eighth speech, Job does not even bother to respond to his friends, whom he has now completely written off due to Eliphaz' ferocious assault. He begins by wishing for access to God, Whom he cannot find (23:1-9). He then asserts that he has maintained his integrity even in the midst of his trials (23:10-17). In 24:1-12, Job complains that men get away with wickedness all the time and the innocent suffer without being avenged, yet God does nothing about it. This is Job's basic dilemma: he understands that the righteous often suffer and the wicked often prosper, but he does not understand why. In 24:13-21, Job describes the rebellious man and how he is brought to death, yet counters this with the observation that the righteous are brought to death as well (24:22-25). Thus, in the end, there is no difference between the fate of the two groups. He ends with a challenge to his friends, which prompts one more response (24:25).

*Bildad's third speech, 25:1-6.* Blidad's third speech is one last brief, feeble attempt to convince Job he is wrong, before the three friends give up entirely on the dialogue. Bildad's argument is that all men are unclean before God, which explains why all die. It is probably implied that Job cannot protest his integrity as strongly as he has. He certainly should not summon Almighty God to a court hearing. However, Bildad still does not give up on the idea that Job is suffering for his sinfulness.

*Job's ninth speech, 26:1–31:40.* Job's ninth speech is his final and climactic utterance. The speech can be divided into three major sections, based on the narrative headings in 26:1, 27:1, and 29:1. Job lays out his case in full in this speech, and he and his three friends feel that they have nothing more to say when it is over. Chapter 26 is introductory, and sets the tone for the rest of the speech. It begins with biting sarcasm directed at Bildad and the other two friends for their total lack of assistance and their false claim to speak wisdom (26:1-4). Rather than simply mock his friends, however, Job intends to teach them true wisdom and truly memorable sayings, thereby proving that his knowledge of God is not in fact inferior to theirs, as well as laying out his worldview in full before applying it to his present situation (cf. 27:11-12). Job begins in 26:5-14 with a stunning affirmation of God's majesty and power with regard to His creation of all things, and His upholding and awareness of the same. These verses are an incredible demonstration of knowledge about the physical world and the structure of the universe—and even of things outside of the universe. Job is really beginning a remembrance of how things used to be, and he begins with an overview of his outlook on God, especially God's system of dealing with men and the hidden things of God.

In chs. 27–28, Job then demonstrates his wisdom by teaching his friends concerning God's ways. In ch. 27, he demonstrates his knowledge of God's treatment of the wicked (27:13-23), though not after first affirming his own righteousness and wishing calamity upon his enemies (27:1-12). Although he has already recognized exceptions to the rule, he here tells his friends that he understands that wickedness does indeed bring calamity. In ch. 28, Job recalls his parable on wisdom, perhaps to make good on his promise to teach his friends concerning God's ways (27:11), or as a recollection of how he got on the right path as a believer. The parable concerns the problem of wisdom. The first paragraph (28:1-11) poetically describes a mining operation which shows man's great skill in bringing forth what is hidden. Yet wisdom is even more difficult to obtain, since it is nowhere to be found in the natural world and cannot be purchased with silver and gold, though it is of more value than any precious metal or gemstone (28:12-22). The solution to the riddle is hinted at in 28:22, which forms a bridge to the final paragraph: man must look outside of his own realm to the One who inhabits eternity, for God alone has seen and understood the pathway to wisdom (28:23-28). Fortunately, God has revealed this pathway to man: wisdom may be found by fearing the Lord and by its counterpoint, departing from evil (28:28).

In chs. 29–31, Job moves from the abstract to the concrete, reflecting on his own personal situation, but continuing, in ch. 29, his remembrance of how things used to be, as he wistfully recalls the happiness of his former state. This is then contrasted in ch. 30 with an overview of his lamentable current condition. Job complains about being derided by society's dregs (30:1-15), about his affliction under the hand of God (30:16-23), and about the injustice and wretchedness of his condition (30:24-31). In ch. 31, Job sets forth the final and definitive asseveration of his integrity. His argument is introduced in 31:1-4 by a statement of what he believes he deserves from God, which is prosperity for righteousness and punishment for unrighteousness. He then proceeds to assert his truthful character (31:5-8), his marital fidelity (31:9-12), his just treatment of his workers (31:13-15), his assistance to vulnerable people (31:16-23), his rejection of idolatry (31:24-28), his purity of heart (31:29-36), and his fair business practices (31:37-40a). Job then rests his case (31:40b).

*Elihu's Speech, 32:1–37-24*

By all appearances, the conversation was now over, and everyone wanted it to be over. But there are two listeners who have yet to speak—Elihu and Yahweh. Elihu was a young but wise bystander who had politely waited to speak until the older men had had their say (32:1-5). However, there was no resolution to their dialogue—they had simply traded false accusations until they grew tired of speaking. Now Elihu, who knew how to apply correct theology to Job's situation, could no longer contain himself. He begins by stating that he had incorrectly assumed that the older men would have the wisdom to answer Job (32:6-10), but since they had found no answer, he would now give an answer unlike theirs (32:11-14). In 32:15-22, Elihu states what he is thinking as he prepares to speak. This section is necessary for Elihu to win the right to be heard by explaining why he is speaking.

In ch. 33, Elihu defends God's dealings with man against Job's accusations. He begins by meekly appealing to Job to hear him out, and to answer him if he can (33:1-7). In 33:8-12, he cites Job's basic error, which is the claim that God is treating him unjustly. Elihu gives his basic answer to Job in 33:12-13: Job has no right to challenge God or to demand that God explain what He is doing, because man is not in a position to hold God accountable or to tell God what to do. In fact, however, God does communicate with man—through dreams (33:14-18) or through chastisement (33:19-22), which, when properly interpreted, leads to man's repentance and restoration (33:23-28). Elihu concludes the first part of his speech by giving Job a chance to respond (33:29-33). For the first time, Job has no answer, and so Elihu continues.

In ch. 34, Elihu vindicates God's justice. First, in 34:1-9, Elihu rebukes Job's claim that God has treated him unrighteously. In 34:10-15, Elihu argues that it is impossible for the One who creates and sustains human life to sin. In 34:16-20, Elihu argues that it is impossible for the One who governs the world to sin. In 34:21-30, Elihu defends God's treatment of the wicked, arguing that God is the perfect Judge because he knows everything men do (34:21-23). God does in fact punish the wicked (34:24-28), and when He appears to remain silent it must be in accord with just purposes which man, in his ignorance, cannot see (34:29-30). Elihu then rebukes Job for challenging God's sovereignty by asserting that he knows how God should treat him better than God does—an act of rebellion against God's rule (34:31-37).

As Elihu proceeds with his speech, he defends God's sovereignty in ch. 35. Since God's Being is impassive—no human or angelic actions have any effect on His Being—He is a neutral as a Judge (35:1-8). God's judgments are self-determined; they are completely uninfluenced by man's attempts to prejudice the judgment, and include no basis for rendering judgment other than the principles of justice themselves. Many men cry out to God to save them when they are in distress, but most do so insincerely—and God, who knows everything, rejects impious prayers (35:9-16). Job's prayer is especially to be rejected because he has openly challenged God. Ironically, Job was complaining that God does not act quickly enough to bring justice, when in fact Job would have been destroyed immediately had God acted immediately (35:16).

Elihu continues to a new topic, defending God's use of affliction (36:1-23). In 36:1-16, Elihu describes God's purposes in bringing affliction—for the wicked, to destroy them, and for the righteous, to refine them. He therefore calls Job to repent, rather than calling to God out of a false pretense or desiring death (36:17-23). God now begins to approach the group in a great tempest, and the remainder of Elihu's speech is occupied with a call to humble oneself before the sovereign God (36:24–37:24). God's awesome power and unfathomable ways make the very thought of a man questioning His course of action totally preposterous. Elihu calls upon Job to magnify God for His awesome majesty, as displayed in the approaching storm (36:24-33). Elihu himself is moved by God's appearance, and describes how the powerful storms of winter display the greatness of God's power (37:1-13). He admonishes Job concerning the absolute impossibility of instructing the God who designed and governs nature (37:14-20). In 37:21-24, Elihu summarizes and concludes his argument, and announces God's arrival. God will proceed to take up Elihu's argument where the latter had left it off. Elihu's speech had prepared the way for God's appearance by showing Job and his friends their error beforehand, thereby readying Job to humble himself before God instead of angrily challenging God.

### God's Speeches, 38:1–41:34

Repeatedly in his speeches, Job had demanded a hearing with God. When God finally appears, however, Job's attitude changes from "If I could talk with God face to face, I would tell him what I think!" to "Wow!" Job realizes that he is nowhere near God's equal, and he is totally overwhelmed by the glory of God. It is ridiculous for Job to be acting as if he can tell God what God should be doing.

It is interesting that although the purpose of suffering is the crux of the whole book, suffering is not even mentioned in the divine discourse. God simply asserts that He knows more than Job, and His prerogatives override Job's. Given this, Job has no right to charge God with injustice for his suffering. God says, "You cannot trace My ways, but you can trust Me." It is not for Job to know the explanation for what God does.

*God's first speech, 38:1–40:2.* In God's first speech, He begins by asserting that Job does not know what he is talking about (38:1-3). To prove this, God demonstrates His knowledge and governance of nature, which Job does not understand. God argues that if Job does not understand the natural world and natural processes, and he does not know how to make the things God made, then he cannot claim that he knows better than God how God should be governing the world and treating Job. God poses more than seventy questions to Job in His two speeches, for which Job has zero answers. In 38:1-38, God demonstrates His creation, governance, and knowledge of inanimate nature: the earth (38:4-7), the sea (38:8-11), light (38:12-15), the unsearchable (36:16-18), natural forces (38:19-24), precipitation (38:25-30), the celestial world (38:31-33), and storms (38:34-38). In 38:39–39:30, God demonstrates His creation, governance, and knowledge of animate nature: young lions and ravens—helpless animals (38:39-41); wild goats—distant animals (39:1-4); the wild ass and the wild ox—untamable animals (39:5-12); the ostrich—a stupid but strong animal (39:13-18); the horse—a steely animal (39:19-25); and the hawk and the eagle—high flying animals (39:26-30). After this dazzling survey of His handiwork, God demands an answer from Job (40:1-2).

*Job's first response 40:3-5.* Job, speaking now for the first time since ch. 31, gives the wrong response. Job says he will not answer God—but God wants an answer. God has asked him if he wants to argue with Him, and Job says he does not. But that was not really the point of the question. Job had been arguing and contending with God for some time before this; therefore what he needed to do was to confess the power of God and the foolishness of his own words, and to humble himself in repentance before God, as in 42:1-6. God wants Job to say, "I was wrong"—not "I won't say anything else."

*God's second speech, 40:6–41:34.* Since Job has not yet expressed repentance, God renews His challenge to Job in 40:6-14. If Job is going to condemn God in order to justify himself, he needs to show that he is in a position that gives him the right to do so. In 40:15–41:34, God boasts about the two most impressive animals He has created in order to show that Job, who is dwarfed by the size and power of these animals, is nowhere near God's equal. It is the extended description of the awesomeness of behemoth and leviathan that finally makes Job drop to his knees and humble himself before Almighty God.

The descriptions of behemoth and leviathan clearly occupy the climactic position in God's argument that He is infinitely greater than Job.[12] Possibly they were not mentioned previously because they were relatively rare in Job's day and lived several days' journey from Job's home region. Behemoth, as will be seen, is the largest sauropod dinosaur, while leviathan is the largest and fiercest pliosaur.

Behemoth is set forth in 40:15-24 as the first of the two great showcases of God's power and skill in the earth. If the language of 40:15-24 is taken literally, it can only refer to a very large herbaceous dinosaur.[13] In fact, when taken at face value, the language describes perfectly a sauropod dinosaur such as Brachiosaurus or Diplodocus. There is therefore no reason to think that the description is anything other than a literal description of the largest dinosaur—unless one has an absolute precommitment, on the basis of Darwinian evolution, to the idea that dinosaurs could not have been alive 4,000 years ago. The description of behemoth as "the chief of the ways of God" (40:19) seems to conclusively prove that behemoth is the largest land animal God ever created, as does the use of the honorific plural בְּהֵמוֹת (*behemoth*) to refer to the largest of all large land animals (בְּהֵמָה).[14]

There is scientific debate as to what was the largest sauropod dinosaur. Brachiosaurus, which was about 85 feet long and 40 feet tall, is the largest dinosaur that has been preserved complete in the fossil record, although the fragmentary remains of Argentinasaurus suggest that it may have been as much as 120 feet long and weighed 100 tons; one of its vertebrae was four feet thick. Possibly there was only a single sauropod "kind" on board the ark, of which the fossils represent the variations of that kind. Behemoth would then be a general term for all sauropods.

Job, who had seen full grown sauropod dinosaurs in person, was staggered by God's vivid depiction of them. Yet there was one more creature God made that was even more powerful and more awe-inspiring than hundred-ton sauropods. Chapter 41 sets forth the great and final showcase of God's might, which is leviathan.[15] If the description of behemoth could be stretched to fit the hippopotamus for those who are sympathetic to a naturalistic view of origins, the same cannot be done with leviathan, for the whole chapter is replete with language which fits no living animal, but which perfectly describes a fire-breathing

---

[12] To suppose that behemoth and leviathan are the hippopotamus or elephant and the crocodile, as most commentators do, would be anticlimactic, to say the least. Even a child can see that these chapters describe a great dinosaur and a fire-breathing dragon.

[13] Hippos and elephants do not have tails like cedar trees (40:17).

[14] בְּהֵמָה is the normal Hebrew word for "beast," referring to cattle and other large land animals, so that the honorific plural would refer to the largest of all beasts.

[15] It is impossible that leviathan was a mythical creature, or that it was intended to be understood as mythical (cf. Ps 104:26). Throughout chs. 38–41, God is boasting of the things He has made to display His power and wisdom. An imaginary creature would reveal nothing about God's power, and exaggerated language would likewise weaken God's case by affirming what was not actually true. Even if someone suggests that the book of Job was made up by a Hebrew writer around the time of the Babylonian exile, such a writer would still have to make an appeal to real creatures to argue his case for God. It should also be noted that everyone agrees that all the animals named before Behemoth and Leviathan are real and are described literally; they only dispute these two because of anti-supernatural theological presuppositions.

dragon. This animal is said to be totally "without his like" on the earth (41:33), being the absolutely fiercest and most indomitable animal in all of creation, and the only fearless one; lions, bears, and armies alike stood no chance of surviving a confrontation with this ferocious dragon.

The Hebrew word transliterated as "leviathan" (לִוְיָתָן) comes from a common Semitic root which has the verbal idea of twisting. "Leviathan" essentially means "twister," and may well have been the original name which Adam gave to this creature. Leviathan was a dinosaur-like creature which lived in the ocean, but which could also come onto land, probably moving by means of flippers on the seashore. Of the two major categories of these creatures, plesiosaurs (long, thin necks, small heads) and pliosaurs (short, thick necks, long heads), the description of leviathan matches the physiology of a pliosaur. The largest species of pliosaur, Kronosaurus, was as much as 55 to 66 feet in length, and weighed up to 50 tons. The skull of the Kronosaurus is a quarter of its entire body length, making its mouth of fearsome proportions. It is evident from the fossilized remains of the Kronosaurus that he was a powerful swimmer (cf. 41:31-32) who would turn and twist powerfully to maneuver.

God begins in 41:1-11 by challenging Job to challenge leviathan. God argues that if no man can stand before leviathan, then certainly no man can stand before the Creator of leviathan. Since Job knew what leviathan was (cf. 3:8), God did not need to begin with a description of leviathan. However, to press the point home, God describes leviathan in vivid detail in 41:12-34. According to 41:18-21, leviathan has fire-producing mechanisms in its mouth and/or nostrils—and, because this is such an impressive weapon, these verses describe it in some eight different ways. It is impossible to tell from a skeleton whether Kronosaurus had a fire-producing mechanism, although there is an enormous cavity under its nostrils which could well have served this purpose; tales of fire-breathing dragons are far too ubiquitous in the folklore of peoples everywhere to seriously doubt their existence.[16] Likewise, the scales or scutes which covered the body of leviathan (41:15-16, 23, 30) apparently have not been preserved in the fossil record.

### *Job's Repentance and Restoration, 42:1-17*

When God finishes describing leviathan, He does not, as previously, need to prompt Job to respond. Job is completely overwhelmed by God's display of power and majesty through this magnificent creature. As soon as there is a break in the monologue, Job speaks again. Now he finally recognizes and admits his mistake and humbles himself before God (42:1-6). He still does not know why he is suffering or why the wicked prosper, but he no longer needs to know—his new awareness of God's power and wisdom makes him comfortable to simply accept God's will for his life and to trust God's governance of the world. He realizes that his accusation that God was mistreating him was a totally ignorant and impious claim concerning matters that can be accurately judged only from a position of omniscience.

God graciously accepted Job's repentance immediately, without any demand for penance or payment. God then turned to Job's three friends, of whom Eliphaz was the ringleader (42:7-9). Although both Elihu and God had directed their speeches primarily at Job, Job's friends had actually spoken worse things concerning God than he. Not only had they harmed their friend, and spoken against God by speaking against God's servant, they had expressed a theology which portrayed Yahweh as a God who, like the idols of the nations, could be manipulated to get what one wants in life. Because Job's three friends had asserted that they possessed considerably more spirituality, wisdom, and stature than Job, God wanted them to actively submit themselves to Job and acknowledge his primacy to demonstrate their repentance. After seeing God, Job's friends wasted no time in getting right with Him.

The narrator completes Job's history by recording the renewal of his prosperity (42:10-17). Apparently it was after Job made intercession for his friends that God finally healed him of his boils. God

---

[16] A dinosaur-like creature that is still living to this day, the komodo dragon, is not only powerful but is also poisonous—something that would never have been guessed from the fossil record.

then gave Job twice as much as he had before[17] and blessed him with a long life of uninterrupted prosperity after the brief period of severe calamity, thereby demonstrating His compassion and mercy (cf. James 5:11).

---

[17] Job's first ten children were not annihilated like his cattle, but were in heaven. God had only to give Job ten more children to give him twice as many.

## Bibliography for Job

Zuck's commentaries are generally good, though he is unclear on the historical setting and denies that behemoth and leviathan are extinct dinosaurs. Larry Waters, who has some good articles on the book of Job in *Bibliotheca Sacra*, likes Zuck's commentaries. The critical commentaries are heavy on redaction criticism and deny the historical setting of the book.

Alden, Robert L. *Job*. New American Commentary 11. Nashville: Broadman & Holman, 1993.
  **Note:** Alden taught at Denver Seminary, which is only weakly evangelical.

Andersen, Francis I. *Job: An Introduction and Commentary*. Tyndale Old Testament Commentaries. London: Inter-Varsity Press, 1976.

Barnes, Albert. *Job*. 2 vols. Notes on the Old Testament. London: Blackie & Son, 1847.
  **Note:** Volume 1 covers chs. 1–21, and vol. 2 covers chs. 22–42.

Clines, David J. A. *Job 1–20*. Word Biblical Commentary 17. Dallas: Word, 1989.
  **Note:** Clines is liberal, and is heavy on redaction criticism.

———. *Job 21–37*. Word Biblical Commentary 18A. Dallas: Word, 2006.

Cook, F. C. "Job." In *The Holy Bible with an Explanatory and Critical Commentary*, ed. F. C. Cook, vol. 4, 1-145. Cambridge: C. J. Clay, 1892.

Davidson, A. B. *The Book of Job: With Notes, Introduction and Appendix*. The Cambridge Bible for Schools and Colleges. Cambridge: Cambridge, 1884.
  **Note:** I believe Davidson is liberal-leaning.

Delitzsch, Franz. *Biblical Commentary on the Book of Job*. 2 vols. Translated by Francis Bolton. Reprint: Grand Rapids: Eerdmans, 1949.
  **Note:** Volume 1 covers chs. 1–21; vol. 2 covers chs. 22–42.

Dhorme, Édouard. *A Commentary on the Book of Job*. Translated by Harold Knight. Nashville: Thomas Nelson, 1967.
  **Note:** Eugene Merrill thinks Dhorme's commentary is the best.

Driver, S. R. *The Book of Job in the Revised Version: With Introductions and Brief Annotations*. Oxford: Clarendon, 1908.

von Ewald, Georg Heinrich August. *Commentary on the Book of Job with Translation*. Translated by J. Frederick Smith. London: Williams and Norgate, 1882.

Green, William Henry. *The Argument of the Book of Job Unfolded*. New York: Hurst, 1891.
  **Note:** Jim Allman recommends this commentary.

Hartley, John E. *The Book of Job*. New International Commentary on the Old Testament. Grand Rapids: Eerdmans, 1988.

Heater, Homer, Jr. *A Septuagint Translation Technique in the Book of Job*. Catholic Biblical Quarterly Monograph Series. Washington, DC: The Catholic Biblical Association of America, 1982.

Kraeling, Emil G. *The Book of the Ways of God*. New York: Charles Scribner's Sons, 1939.
    **Note:** Kraeling is liberal, but the title of his work is right on target.

Pope, Marvin H. *Job: Introduction, Translation, and Notes*. 3rd ed. Anchor Bible. Garden City, NY: Doubleday & Company, 1973.

Reyburn, William D. *A Handbook on the Book of Job*. UBS Handbook Series. New York: United Bible Societies, 1992.

Ridout, S. *The Book of Job*. New York: Loizeaux, 1919.

Simonetti, Manlio, Marco Conti, and Thomas C. Oden, eds. *Job*. Ancient Christian Commentary on Scripture: Old Testament, vol. 7. Downers Grove, IL: InterVarsity Press, 2006.

Smick, Elmer B. "Job." Pages 841-1060 in *The Expositor's Bible Commentary*, vol. 4. Grand Rapids: Zondervan, 1988.

———. "Job." Revised by Tremper Longman III. Pages 675-921 in *The Expositor's Bible Commentary: Revised Edition*, vol. 4, edited by Tremper Longman III and David E. Garland. Grand Rapids: Zondervan, 2010.

Thomas, David. *Book of Job: Expository and Homiletical Commentary*. Grand Rapids: Kregel, 1982. Originally published as *Problemata Mundi*. 2nd ed. London: Smith, Elder, 1878.

Wilson, Gerald H. *Job*. New International Biblical Commentary. Peabody, MA: Hendrickson, 2007.

Zuck, Roy B. *Job*. Chicago: Moody Press, 1978.
    **Note:** Larry Waters likes Zuck's commentary.

Zuck, Roy B. "Job." Pages 715-777 in *The Bible Knowledge Commentary: Old Testament*, ed. John F. Walvoord and Roy B. Zuck. Colorado Springs: Chariot Victor, 1985.

Zuck, Roy B., ed. *Sitting with Job: Selected Studies on the Book of Job*. Grand Rapids: Baker, 1992.
    **Note:** Many of the contributors are liberal, though there are also many conservative contributors. Some people highly recommend Gregory Parsons' articles, but I am not so sure.

# Interpretive Guide to the Psalms

The Psalms are, as a group, certainly one of the best known portions of the Bible.[1] They have rightly been called a window into Israel's faith,[2] since they allow us to hear and feel the deep personal piety and religious devotion of individual Israelites in ancient times. Yet the Psalms have also been a favorite of Christians throughout the Church Age for the unmatched expression which they give to the believer's religious feelings in all the situations of life, as well for public worship as for private meditation. No book of the Old Testament is so frequently quoted in the New, and more Christian commentators have written on the Psalms than on any other OT book.

> The Psalms are an epitome of the Bible, adapted to the purposes of devotion. . . . They are, for this purpose, adorned with the figures, and set off with all the graces, of poetry; the poetry itself is designed yet farther to be recommended by the charms of music, thus consecrated to the service of God: that so delight may prepare the way for improvement, and pleasure become the handmaid of wisdom, while every turbulent passion is calmed by sacred melody, and the evil spirit is still dispossessed by the harp of the son of Jesse. This little volume, like the paradise of Eden, affords us in perfection, though in miniature, every thing that groweth elsewhere, every tree that is pleasant to the sight, and good for food; and above all, what was there lost, but is here restored—*the tree of life in the midst of the garden.* That which we read, as a matter of speculation, in the other Scriptures, is reduced to practice, when we recite it in the Psalms; in those, repentance and faith are described, but in these they are acted: by a perusal of the former, we learn how others served God, but, by using the latter, we serve him ourselves.
>
> What is there necessary for man to know, which the psalms are not able to teach? They are to beginners an easy and familiar introduction, a mighty augmentation of all virtue and knowledge in such as are entered before, a strong confirmation to the most perfect among others. Heroical magnanimity, exquisite justice, grave moderation, exact wisdom, repentance unfeigned, unwearied patience, the mysteries of God, the sufferings of Christ, the terrors of wrath, the comforts of grace, the works of Providence over this world, and the promised joys of that world which is to come, all good necessarily to be either known, or done, or had, this one celestial fountain yieldeth. Let there be any grief or disease incident unto the soul of man, any wound or sickness named, for which there is not, in this treasure-house, a present comfortable remedy at all times ready to be found.
>
> In the language of this divine book, therefore, the prayers and praises of the church have been offered up to the throne of grace, from age to age. And it appears to have been the manual of the Son of God, in the days of his flesh; who, at the conclusion of his last supper, is generally supposed, and that upon good grounds, to have sung an hymn taken from it; who pronounced, on the cross, the beginning of the twenty-second psalm, 'My God, my God, why hast thou forsaken me?' and expired, with a part of the thirty-first psalm in his mouth, 'Into thy hands I commend my spirit.' Thus He, who had not the Spirit by measure, in whom were hidden all the treasures of wisdom and knowledge, and who spake as never man spake, yet chose to conclude his life, to solace himself in his greatest agony, and at last to breathe out his soul, in the psalmist's form of words, rather than his own. No tongue of man or angel can convey an higher idea of any book, and of their felicity who use it aright.[3]

---

[1] According to common convention, "psalm" should be lowercase except when used with a number, while "Psalmist" should be capitalized. The only drawback to this convention is that the distinction between inspired psalms and non-canonical psalms can only be ascertained from the context. When the Book of Psalms is referenced, the term should be capitalized.

[2] Willem A. VanGemeren, "Psalms" (in *The Expositor's Bible Commentary: Revised Edition*, vol. 5; Grand Rapids: Zondervan, 2008), 23.

The Psalms were Israel's hymnbook, though Israel's worship surely was not restricted to the biblical psalms; no such restriction can be found in the Bible. A study of the Psalms from the biblical text alone is extremely rich theologically, but when set to the proper music, they capture heart and mind in a way that mere speech cannot. Luther once said, "Let others write the theology; let me write the music." The words of the Psalms, like the words of all godly music, have a vital teaching role in the ministry of the church. Nevertheless, the Holy Spirit did not think it fit to preserve for us in the sacred writings musical scores of the Psalms, but the words only, implying that there is not one musical expression alone which can be given to each psalm; rather, believers of later generations are free to compose their own tunes appropriate to Israel's hymnbook. The selection and performance of tunes, including the instruments chosen to be used in the performance, is no inconsequential issue, as the "worship wars" of the modern church well attest: music has a potent effect on human emotions and behavior, and can be good or evil.[4]

Many of the Psalms apply specifically to the situation of the Psalmist, but were nevertheless sung by those to whom they may not have applied directly in a particular time or place. Some of the psalm titles give clues as to why this was done: "to teach" (Ps 60); "to bring to remembrance" (Pss 38, 70); "a prayer of the afflicted, when he is overwhelmed, and poureth out his complaint before Yahweh" (Ps 102). Even Psalm 51, in which David prays for forgiveness from bloodguiltiness, is said in the superscription to have been written for the Chief Musician. There is something in the spirit of these Psalms that we can relate to, and that instructs us, even if we cannot affirm for ourselves everything that the speaker in the psalm affirms for himself. The singers find identity with historic faith, and affirm the spirit of their prayers. For this reason, they are sung, and not just spoken. The Psalms are also sung as a remembrance of God's acts, and of His gracious dealings with men.

All of the Psalms had a historical function in Israel's worship, but this does not by any means imply that every psalm must be describing historical events in the Psalmist's own time. A prophecy could be sung as a hymn, and the people could look to its fulfillment in worship—even if they did not entirely understand what they sang. Prophetic psalms usually have a near term message, as well: Ps 2:10-12 addresses the kings of David's own time with a warning in view of the prophecy; in Ps 110:1, David is noted as the speaker, and he calls the Messiah "my Lord" (present); Ps 95:7c-11 calls upon the Psalmist's contemporaries to get saved so as to enter the future kingdom of which he has just spoken.

## Authorship

The book of Psalms is a compilation of works by individual authors, with Ezra likely being the final compiler. Two-thirds of the psalms contain superscriptions which identify an author, as follows:

*Ascriptions of the Psalms in the MT*

David.................................................... 73

---

[3] Thomas Hartwell Horne, *An Introduction to the Critical Study and Knowledge of the Holy Scriptures* (9th ed.; London: Longman, Brown, Green, and Longmans, 1846), 4:115-16. The second paragraph is a quotation from a certain Hooker.

[4] At some point in the history of Protestantism, most churches stopped using Psalters, and for this reason many or most Christians today are completely unaware that all the psalms have been versified and set to music in a variety of ways in English Psalters since the Reformation. Psalters also exist in many other languages besides English. Probably the best English Psalter is the *Trinity Psalter*; also worth noting is *The Book of Psalms for Singing*. To my knowledge, no attempt has been made to set the Psalms to music in English without altering the biblical text. To do so would require the use of a chant, rather than the usual metrical score.

Asaph ...................................................... 12
Sons of Korah ...................................... 10
Sons of Korah/Heman .......................... 1
Solomon .................................................. 2
Moses ...................................................... 1
Ethan ...................................................... 1
Unsigned ............................................. 50

These ascriptions, it should be noted, are part of the Hebrew text of the Psalms, although in many English Bibles they are almost indistinguishable from headings added by editors, and many readers are not aware of the difference.

Critical scholars, who do not believe in the inspiration of the Bible, freely deny the accuracy of the superscriptions. Many evangelicals are influenced by higher criticism, and have followed suit. Since denying the superscription removes the key to the historical setting of the psalm, commentators then speculate about what the setting may have been, and often assign different speakers to different sections of the psalms in a supposed dialogue—even though new speakers are almost never introduced or noted through a change of person, and when they are it is still a single author who is narrating what they say.

There is in fact strong evidence for the authenticity of the psalm titles in the MT.[5] They are contained in every Hebrew manuscript, including the Dead Sea Scrolls; for example, 11QPs[a] has the titles consistently, and in line with the main text, not separated from it. Matthew 22:43-46 shows that the attribution of Psalm 110 to David was completely unquestioned by the Pharisees at the time of Jesus, for Jesus' argument for the OT affirmation of the divinity of the Messiah is hinged on this attribution. Archer notes that the Hebrew psalm titles often point to a historical situation different from what a later rabbi would guess without the title, and some even note a historical background that is not explicitly noted in the OT historical books.[6] Conversely, some of the psalms with the greatest number of historical allusions have no superscription, when these would be the ones most likely to have superscriptions spuriously added by later rabbis. Archer also points out that by the second century B.C., the meaning of technical terms in many of the psalm titles were unknown to the LXX translators, implying that the titles had been created in the ancient past.[7]

Some scholars argue that some of the psalms, like the song of Habakkuk 3, originally had both a prescript and a postscript, and that parts of the titles which were originally postscripts ("to the chief musician," the melody, and the instrumentation) were incorrectly transferred to the following psalms.[8] While this certainly is a thesis worth researching, for the purposes of this study the psalm titles will be considered correct as they stand in the MT.

## *Authors of the Psalms*

Each of the known authors of the psalms occupied a prophetic office. David and Solomon both prophesied as persons who were specially anointed by Yahweh and were in the messianic line. The temple singers, such as Asaph and the sons of Korah, likewise occupied a prophetic office (1 Chr 25:1; 2

---

[5] The LXX ascriptions are probably mostly worthless guesses, though the LXX ascription of Ps 95 is apparently cited in Heb 4:7.

[6] Gleason L. Archer, Jr. *A Survey of Old Testament Introduction* (Chicago: Moody Press, 1964), 428.

[7] Ibid., 429.

[8] Ibid., 434; James William Thirtle, *The Titles of the Psalms: Their Nature and Meaning Explained* (2nd ed.; New York: Henry Frowde, 1905).

Chr 29:30). Moses obviously did as well. Thus, the unknown authors of psalms must have also occupied a prophetic office—most likely, as temple singers. In reality, most or all of the unsigned psalms were written by the same persons or groups as the signed psalms.

*David.* Nearly half of the psalms are attributed to David, Israel's paradigmatic king, and David was surely the author of many of the anonymous psalms.[9] All five books of the Psalter contain Davidic psalms, though Book I (Pss 1–41) is exclusively Davidic.[10]

Whereas Moses was Israel's great lawgiver, David was Israel's great poet and musician. It was David who first organized temple worship, and his psalms set the standard for all future compositions. Rolled up in this one person were a stunning combination of traits which made him the ideal Psalmist: a righteous heart, a mind of wisdom, musical skill, full experience of all of life's trials and triumphs, leadership of the nation of Israel, the promise of messianic redemption, the founding of Jerusalem, a unique ability to give fitting expression to emotion, and the inspiration of the Holy Spirit. If anyone should doubt from the historical record of David's moral failures whether he was a righteous man, the psalms which he left unambiguously testify to the purity and holiness of his heart. It likewise becomes clear from a study of his psalms that David was a man of great faith. No matter how dark the danger, David always prayed in confidence that God would hear him, and usually ended his prayers with a great burst of thanksgiving in anticipation of the answer.

In the Old Testament, prophets were indwelt by the Holy Spirit, but normal people were not. The Holy Spirit came upon David as a youth (1 Sam 16:13), and this gave him a prophetic function thereafter. As a prophet, David was able and qualified to write Scripture, and to compose prophetic psalms.

*Asaph.* After David, the largest number of ascriptions, twelve, name Asaph as the author (Pss 50, 73–83). Asaph, a descendant of Levi in the family of Gershon, was appointed by David as the chief Levitical singer when David brought the ark to Jerusalem (1 Chr 16:4-7). Asaph was thus like the senior minister of music under David, leading and supervising the temple musicians, and he was still leading worship at the dedication of Solomon's temple (2 Chr 5:12). Asaph's sons ministered with him as early as the reign of David, and his descendants are mentioned as retaining a position of prominence in temple worship right through the monarchic period and continuing after the exile (Ezra 3:10; Neh 11:22). The temple musicians are said to "prophesy" in 1 Chr 25:1-3, and Asaph is called "the seer" (הַחֹזֶה) in 2 Chr 29:30. The psalms of Asaph contain some of the most difficult Hebrew in the Psalter, demonstrating Asaph's skill with the archaic form of the Hebrew language. Doubtless Asaph drew inspiration for his work from David's example and instruction, though he also reports prophetic visions of his own in keeping with his own role as a seer.

*The sons of Korah.* The sons (i.e., descendants) of Korah wrote Psalms 42–49, 84–85, and 87–89 (note that Heman the Ezrahite and Ethan the Ezrahite were associated with the sons of Korah; also, Psalm 43 bears no superscription, but is a continuation of Psalm 42.).[11] Korah was a patriarch of a Levitical family within the Kohathite clan (Num 26:58; 1 Chr 9:19) who died when he led a rebellion against

---

[9] Davidic psalms have a certain style that one seems to recognize after a while, although this is hard to quantify.

[10] Note that the phrase מִזְמוֹר לְדָוִד means "A Psalm *of* David," not "A Psalm *for* David." The לְ is needed to make the word "psalm" indefinite in the genitive construction. Without the לְ, it would mean "The Psalm of David," as if David only wrote one psalm. It cannot be doubted that at least some of the psalms entitled לְדָוִד were written by David, which confirms the meaning of the expression.

[11] For references to Heman and Ethan, see 1 Kgs 4:31; 1 Chr 2:6; 15:17, 19.

Moses in the wilderness (Num 16), though his sons did not join in his rebellion and therefore did not die with him (Num 26:11). David appointed the Korahites for service in the tabernacle (1 Chr 26:1, 19), and they are later noted as leading temple worship (2 Chr 20:19). Fourteen of the twenty-four orders of singers appointed by David in 1 Chr 25 were comprised of descendants of Korah. Many of the psalms of Korah must have been written at the time of David, but some, especially the unsigned psalms, could have been written much later.

*Solomon.* Psalms 72, 127, and 132 (unsigned) are Solomonic. Solomon, as the wisest man who ever lived, composed 1,005 songs (1 Kgs 4:32). However, only a few of his songs have been preserved in Scripture, probably because of his rebellion at the end of his life. The language and beauty of the Solomonic psalms is of the highest level.

*Moses.* Moses, who wrote Israel's first recorded songs (Exod 15; Deut 32), also left one composition that has been preserved in the Psalter, Psalm 90.

*Others.* The authors of many of the unsigned psalms can be determined with a fair degree of certainty, though in some instances no firm conclusions can be drawn. In most or all instances, these authors are the same as those of the signed psalms. It is notable that not one of the 150 psalms was composed by a woman. This is in contrast to modern hymns and choruses, in which women are very well represented. The biblical model, however, is for every hymn in the church's hymnal to be written by men, since women are not to teach in the church, and writing a hymn is a form of teaching. It is also noteworthy that every canonical psalm was written by a true believer. Once again, evangelical hymnody is found to be careless at this point, since several well-known hymns (e.g., "Come Thou Fount of Every Blessing") were written by people who apostatized or who held to heretical theology.

## Date

Each psalm is an independent composition, to be assigned its own date. Thus, the dating of various psalms is best discussed under those individuals psalms, though for many psalms the date of composition is uncertain. Known dates of composition range from about 1405 B.C. (Ps 90) to 535 B.C. (Ps 126). Individual psalms were composed at least as early as Moses (Ps 90), and as late as the exile (Ps 137) or afterward (Ps 126). The final addition to the Psalter was likely made by Ezra around 400 B.C. The majority of psalms were composed during the time of David, from about 1020 to 970 B.C.

Before the discovery of the Dead Sea Scrolls, it was popular for liberals to suggest that many of the psalms were composed in the Maccabean period. The Scrolls have proved that the psalms had to have been written much earlier. The books of Malachi and Chronicles are intended to close the OT canon, and Malachi represents himself as the final writing prophet before the Messiah, so the Psalter must have reached its final canonical form shortly before the writing of Malachi.

## Arrangement and Classification of the Psalms

Although the Psalms comprise a single book, they were anciently divided into five "books," or sections. This fivefold division in all likelihood reflects five stages in the process of the compilation of the Psalter, as more psalms were composed and added over time by inspired compilers.[12] Each of the first

---

[12] Some suggest that the five books of the Psalter correspond to the five books of the Pentateuch, and that the character of the psalms in each book correspond to the character of each book of the Pentateuch. However, the Torah was probably not divided into five books until the intertestamental period, though of course the five major

four books of the Psalter is distinctly marked by a closing doxology (41:13; 72:18-19; 89:52; 106:48), while the whole of Psalm 150 is like a doxology. On this basis, the Psalms can be outlined as follows:

I.  Book I – Psalms 1–41 – Psalms of David (Personal Emphasis)
II.  Book II – Psalms 42–72 – Psalms for the Chief Musician
    A. Psalms of the sons of Korah – 42–49
    B. Psalm of Asaph – 50
    C. Psalms of David – 51–71
        1. Psalm 51
        2. Maskils of David 52–55
        3. Miktams of David 56–60
        4. Psalms 61–64
        5. Psalm-Songs of David 65–68
        6. Psalms 69–71
    D. Psalm of Solomon – 72
III.  Book III – Psalms 73–89 – Psalms by the Temple Singers
    A. Psalms of Asaph – 73–83
    B. Psalms of the sons of Korah – 84–85
    C. Psalm of David – 86
    D. Psalms of the sons of Korah – 87–89
IV.  Book IV – Psalms 90–106 – Psalms of God's Care for Israel
    A. Psalms of rest in God – 90–92
    B. Psalms of the messianic kingdom – 93–100
    C. Psalm of the king's righteous rule 101
    D. Prayer for mercy on Zion 102
    E. Hallelujah Psalms – 103–106
V.  Book V – Psalms 107–150 – Psalms for Special Liturgical Use
    A. Psalms of deliverance (Davidic) 107–110
    B. Acrostic Psalms 111–112
    C. Hallel Psalms – 113–118
    D. An acrostic meditation on the Law of God – 119
    E. Songs of Ascent – 120–134
    F. Psalms of Israel's history – 135–137
    G. Psalms of God's care for David – 138–145
    H. Hallelujah Psalms – 146–150

Book I (Pss 1–41) consists entirely of psalms of David, assuming that the four unsigned psalms in this group (1, 2, 10, 33) are Davidic due to their association with a collection of Davidic psalms.[13] This collection was almost certainly originally made by David.

Book II (Pss 42–72) consists almost entirely of psalms for the chief musician. Out of Pss 42–72, the only ones which are not explicitly dedicated to the chief musician by the superscription are 43, 48, 50, 63,

---

units of the Torah could have be identified beforehand. Parallels between the Pentateuch and the Psalter may be coincidental or illusory.

[13] The first two psalms are introductory and so need no superscription (Ps 2 is said to be Davidic in Acts 4:25), while the tenth psalm is a continuation of the ninth. Psalm 33 may lack a title by a transcriptional accident, or because it is closely connected to Ps 32; at any rate, it is clear by its placement in the middle of the Davidic psalms in Book I that it must be Davidic. It is possible that the attribution of Davidic authorship of Ps 2 in Acts 4:25 is a reflection of a general belief in the first century A.D. that all the psalms of Book I are Davidic.

71, and 72. It may be fairly assumed that the lack of the superscription does not mean that these psalms were not written for the chief musician, given their placement in a collection with other psalms for the chief musician. Psalm 72:20, "The prayers of David the son of Jesse are ended," is an editorial note which was probably added by the original compiler of Book II to indicate that there were no more Davidic (or Solomonic) psalms in the collection which he was organizing (cf. Job 31:40; Jer 51:64b). If this is the case, then all of Pss 1–72 would be very early, not later than Solomonic times. The addition of further Davidic psalms after the original compilation of the work has a parallel in Prov 25:1. The compiler of Book II could have been Solomon or one of the temple singers.

Book II is comprised mainly of psalms of the sons of Korah (42–49) and Davidic psalms (51–71). Both of these groups of psalms contain various themes, but emphasize God's judgment of the wicked. A single psalm of Asaph (50) separates these sections and forms a hinge between them by describing God's judgment of His own people. Book II is fittingly concluded by a beautiful psalm of Solomon (72), which describes the righteous king's judgment of all the earth.

The authors of Book II are fitting for a collection written for the chief musician. The sons of Korah were the main group of temple singers, so most or all of their songs would be for the chief musician. Asaph actually was the chief musician, so it is natural that one of his psalms should be included in the book of psalms to the chief musician. David was Israel's greatest musician and king, and was closely associated with the temple singers; Solomon was the son of David and the wisest man who ever lived.

Book III (Pss 73–89) consists entirely of psalms by the temple singers—Asaph, their leader under David, and the Korahites. There is one psalm in this collection by David (Ps 86), who was closely associated with the temple singers (cf. 1 Chr 15:27). It is unclear when Book III was compiled, though it is unlikely that it was compiled at the same time as Book II, given the note in Ps 72:20 and the presence of a Davidic psalm in Book III. The majority of psalms in this collection were written by David or his contemporaries (Asaph, Heman, Ethan), although the psalms attributed to the sons of Korah (Pss 84–85, 87) are more difficult to date. Psalm 87 is one of only two psalms in the Psalter which mentions Babylon, though in context the Psalmist is naming distant countries and does not assert that Babylon was a world power in his day. Perhaps this collection was made during the revival instituted at the time of Jehoshaphat or Joash. It could have been compiled by temple singers (the sons of Korah), by the high priest Jehoiada, by the prophet Joel, by Elijah or Elisha, or by some other prophet.

Most of the psalms in Books IV and V are unsigned, though it is very likely that their compiler(s) knew who wrote them. Both books seem to reflect later concerns; the theme of Book IV is God's care for Israel, and possibly was added to the earlier collections at the time of Hezekiah by the prophet Isaiah. Book V contains the only clear exilic psalm (137) and the only clear postexilic psalm (126), and must represent the final inspired addition of psalms to the previous collections. The psalms of Book V seem intended for special liturgical use, reflecting the renewed concern for temple worship and organization under Ezra and Nehemiah. This book must be the product of Ezra's prodigious scribal activity as he was led to bring closure to the OT canon around 400 B.C.

## The Order of the Psalms

As the above outline shows, there is a clearly ordered macrostructure to the Psalms. Though each psalm is an independent composition, the collection is arranged according to complex but logical principles. However, while the above outline identifies major blocks of material, it does not address more detailed questions, such as why Psalm 1 is placed first in the Psalter, or why the Davidic psalms in Book I are placed in their present order, or why other Davidic psalms are not included in Book I. Clearly the order of psalms in the Psalter is just as inspired as the individual psalms themselves, and inspired compilers were responsible for it. Probably the compiler of each of the five books of the Psalms was responsible for the order of the psalms within his book, so that the final inspired compiler, Ezra, was likely only responsible for the arrangement of Book V. That the canonical order of the Psalter is ancient is demonstrated by the antiquity of the manuscript tradition, and also by statements in early rabbinic literature which demonstrate that the logic of the canonical order was not understood by the rabbis.

Some writers think that the Psalter is in disarray in its canonical order, and that there was a more ancient order that was superior. In antiquity, some Christian and Jewish writers complained that the Psalms were not in chronological order. In the early twentieth century, the influential German liberal Hermann Gunkel denied all order and connectivity in the canonical Psalter based on his own form-critical analysis: for any given form-critical category, the psalms in that category were scattered throughout the Psalter, rather than being grouped together. Gunkel viewed these categories so rigidly that he did not see the possibility of connectivity between psalms of different forms. Such views have, however, been challenged by works both new and old.[14] Detailed studies have shown that there are literary and theological links between consecutive psalms, and there is an overall logical flow in the Psalter. For example, Psalms 1 and 2 are closely related, and Psalm 3 is related to Psalms 1–2. Psalms 87–89 are surprisingly coherent, but generically different. Psalms 22 and 23 contrast divine abandonment with divine presence. The royal messianic psalms (2, 72, 89) occupy key structural positions in the Psalter. Many other examples could be cited.

While it is certain that there is a logical explanation for the order of the entire Psalter, and that there are overall organizing principles, most of the work that has been done to date has focused on connections between individual psalms, and has not tried to find the link between each psalm all the way through the Psalter or to show an overall flow of thought. As such a project would require an extraordinary amount of original research, no grand argument of the Psalter will be presented here.

### *Classifying the Psalms*

Many systems of classifying the Psalms have been proposed from antiquity until the present, though for modern liberal-critical scholars, Gunkel's form-critical classification based on a hypothetical life setting (*Sitz im Leben*) set the standard (*Ausgewählte Psalmen*, 1904). It should be noted that Gunkel's classification scheme was based on anti-supernaturalist presuppositions, and viewed the psalms as solely a human product, and often a communal product, with reference solely to (late) contemporary events, not to future prophecy or to events early in Israel's history. Following Gunkel's form-critical analysis will tend to consciously or subconsciously discredit the divine origin and historicity of the Psalms. Form criticism also tends to force each psalm into a particular form critical category, analyzing it according to the supposed characteristics of that category, rather than allowing the psalm to define itself. Labeling a psalm according to a certain form-critical category also tends to obscure the connections between it and surrounding psalms of different categories, as has already been noted.

On the other hand, there have been many systems of classification proposed by those who firmly believe in the Bible's divine origin. For example, Luther divided the Psalms into five categories: prophecies about Christ, doctrinal psalms, psalms of comfort, prayer psalms, and psalms of thanksgiving. Horne, writing in the mid-nineteenth century, classified all the psalms under six headings, with subheadings under each: (1) prayers; (2) psalms of thanksgiving; (3) psalms of praise and adoration, displaying the attributes of God; (4) instructive psalms; (5) psalms more eminently and directly prophetical; and (6) historical psalms.[15] However, a later edition of his work contains the following

---

[14] See especially John Forbes, *Studies on the Book of Psalms: The Structural Connection of the Book of Psalms, Both in Single Psalms and in the Psalter as an Organic Whole* (James Forrest, ed.; Edinburgh: T. & T. Clark, 1888); Robert Cole, "The Composition of the Psalter and the Folly of Form Criticism" (paper presented at the annual meeting of the ETS, New Orleans, LA, Nov 19, 2009).

[15] Thomas Hartwell Horne, *An Introduction to the Critical Study and Knowledge of the Holy Scriptures* (9th ed.; London: Longman, Brown, Green, and Longmans, 1846), 4:118-19.

caveat: "the contents are so varied, the transitions from one method to another so sudden, the changes of feeling and expression so rapid, that the different poems cannot be strictly classified."[16]

When one looks to the biblical text itself, many psalms do have labels which are generic classifications of sorts. The term מִזְמוֹר (*psalm*), which occurs fifty-seven times in psalm titles, refers to a song with instrumental accompaniment. The term שִׁיר (*song*), which occurs twenty-seven times in psalm titles, is simply a general term for vocal music. The term שִׁיר הַמַּעֲלוֹת (*song of ascents*) occurs fifteen times in psalm titles, all in a single collection (Pss 120–134). These songs were apparently used in the liturgy of the second temple after the exile, presumably as the temple singers made their way up the steps of the temple complex. Five psalms are titled as a תְּפִלָּה (*prayer*). Five are titled תְּהִלָּה (*praise*). Psalm 100 is titled תּוֹדָה (*thanksgiving*). The meanings of the terms מַשְׂכִּיל (*Maschil/Maskil*, used thirteen times), מִכְתָּם (*Michtam/Miktam*, used six times), and שִׁגָּיוֹן (*Shiggaion*; Ps 7 and Hab 3) are disputed, and so are often transliterated.[17] However, other than the songs of ascents, none of these labels is very helpful for the purposes of classification, since they are do not define mutually exclusive categories—often two of these terms appear in the same title.

Although most modern writers attempt to categorize the Psalms according to some generic classification scheme, such classifications generally fail to recognize the mixture of material in individual psalms, as well as the amount of variety within the Psalter. Because most psalms contain a mixture of content, and the expression of this content is quite varied, no generic classification will be presented here. Instead, the subject of each psalm will be stated independently, so as to allow the text to speak for itself rather than being read through a predefined category.

## The Concept of Hebrew Poetry

The book of Psalms epitomizes what is called "Hebrew poetry," although modern critical scholars now classify almost all non-narrative sections of the OT as "poetry." But what is called "poetry" in Hebrew is far different from what is called "poetry" in English, and it is questionable whether the English term, and the concept associated with it, is properly applicable to the Hebrew psalms.

### *Characteristics of Hebrew "Poetry"*

The primary characteristic of Hebrew "poetry," if the term may be so used, is a literary structure called "parallelism," in which each poetic line is divided into two, occasionally three, corresponding units called "cola" (sg. "colon"). The cola tend to be terse, and the second one complements the thought of the first. In modern English Bibles, poetry is visually represented by placing parallel cola on separate lines, sometimes with the second colon indented underneath the first.

In English, poetry is marked primarily by rhyme, and secondarily by meter. If one hears rhyming verse, he immediately identifies it as poetry. But while in English poetry the lines are supposed to rhyme in sound, in Hebrew poetry it could be said that the lines are supposed to rhyme in thought. In English,

---

[16] Samuel Davidson, *The Text of the Old Testament Considered: With a Treatise on Sacred Interpretation; and a Brief Introduction to the Old Testament Books and the Apocrypha*, vol. 2 of Thomas Hartwell Horne, *An Introduction to the Critical Study and Knowledge of the Holy Scriptures* (10th ed.; Thomas Hartwell Horne, Samuel Davidson, and Samuel Prideaux Tragelles, eds.; London: Longman, Brown, Green, Longmans, & Roberts, 1856), 2:737.

[17] See discussion below, under "Interpretive Issues."

some people dislike poetry because rhyming words are often "cute" but dumb or nonsensical. But in Hebrew, it has to make sense to be poetry.

The conception of Hebrew poetry in the world of biblical scholarship has been shaped in large measure by Robert Lowth's 1753/1763 work *De sacra poesi Hebraeorum*.[18] Although the parallelistic structure of Hebrew poetry has been recognized since ancient times, Lowth gave it more definition and clarity. He identified three categories of parallelism: synonymous, antethetical, and synthetic. Lowth and most scholars who followed him saw the majority of parallelism as synonymous—the second colon simply repeats the first in different words. Pederson sums up this view: "[the Hebrew poet] expresses his thought twice in a different manner. . . . He repeats and repeats."[19] In antethetical parallelism, the second colon states something opposite to the first, while synthetic parallelism is a catch-all term Lowth used for examples that did not fit his other two categories.[20]

James Kugel seriously challenged the prevailing view of Hebrew poetry in his 1981 work *The Idea of Biblical Poetry*. Kugel described the relationship between the first colon (A) and the second colon (B) as "A is so, and *what's more*, B."[21] Kugel rejected Lowth's tripartite classification of parallel lines, instead claiming that all parallelism is synthetic in the sense that B is a continuation of A.[22] There are a great variety of ways in which B continues A, but it is rare that B merely restates A. Lumping all poetic lines into one of a handful of categories tends to overlook the differences between them.

The relationship of B to A is sometimes described as "B sharpens A," since B usually refines the idea in A. By itself, B is not always a sharper image, but it often is. The poet will often omit the verb in B ("verb gapping"), which results in the verbal idea of A being understood in B, and allows the poet to add another descriptive word in B without upsetting the balance[23] of the poetic line. The interpreter of Scripture should pay attention to this to see what the difference between the two lines is, and what interpretational significance this might have. Of course, there is a danger of reading too much into the second colon if one insists it must always be a sharper, different image than the first. A balance must be maintained between the two extremes of seeing the second colon as a simple restatement of the first, and of seeing the two cola as having totally separate significance. It is important for the Bible teacher to communicate this to laymen, so people do not misunderstand parallelism according to one of these extremes.

The language of Hebrew poetry is characterized by terseness, in spite of the parallelistic structure which seems to some to add duplicative material; short statements are prized over longer ones. Poetry frequently omits prepositions, and has fewer occurrences of אֲשֶׁר, אֶת, and הַ. Participles are used more frequently in poetry, especially as substantival personal references. Poetry often has different word order than narrative, and tends to use older vocabulary and linguistic forms. Hebrew narrative normally follows a word order of verb-subject-object, but this is often not the norm in poetry.

---

[18] James Kugel, *The Idea of Biblical Poetry: Parallelism and Its History* (Baltimore: Johns Hopkins UP, 1981), 12.

[19] Johannes Pederson, *Israel: Its Life and Culture* (London, 1926), 123.

[20] Kugel, *The Idea of Biblical Poetry*, 12.

[21] Ibid., 1.

[22] Ibid., 57-58.

[23] Due to the parallelistic nature of Hebrew poetry, the cola are generally of a similar length and syllable count. It should be noted, though, that the biblical authors were not bound by the notion that their lines were required to have precise syllabic balance. Too often, commentators and the editors of BHS propose emendations to the Hebrew text or challenge the Masoretic accentuation solely to create syllabic balance between parallel cola. The primary criteria for colon division should be logical thought units and the Masoretic accentuation, not syllable count.

Beyond parallelism and balance, there are a variety of poetic devices used in the OT. Perhaps the most clearly structured of these is the alphabetic acrostic. An acrostic poem is a poem in which the initial letters of each line or unit, when taken together, spell something meaningful. An alphabetic acrostic starts with the first letter of the alphabet, and each successive line or unit begins with each successive letter, until the alphabet is finished. The following biblical texts are structured as alphabetic acrostics: Pss 9–10; 25; 34; 111; 112; 119; 145; Prov 31:10-31; and Lam 1–4. Ironically, the structure of the acrostic often weakens or replaces the more normative features of poetry, parallelism and balance.[24]

### *The Idea of Hebrew Poetry*

Most scholars since Lowth have accepted the idea that, vis-à-vis the Hebrew OT, "parallelism is poetry."[25] However, Kugel has demonstrated through numerous examples that parallelism is really just a characteristic of elevated Hebrew style, and can be present—or lacking—in any OT genre or composition.[26] The division of the biblical text into the two categories of "poetry" and "prose" has resulted in forced parallelism where there is none in supposedly "poetic" passages, and, conversely, in a failure to recognize parallelism in "prose" passages.[27] Further, where clear parallelistic lines are recognized in "prose" sections, some scholars label these as "poetic fragments" that were inserted into the narrative from another source.[28] In short, the equation between parallelism and poetry has led Bible scholars to impose a rigid structure onto texts that were not bound by such hard-and-fast literary rules. The division of the text into the two categories of "poetry" and "prose" does not leave room for the vast middle ground that lies between the most elevated and structured language in the OT and its plainest, simplest language. Texts are marked as one or the other, and then the supposed structure and features of this writing style are imposed upon the text.

Another weakness with the equation between "poetry" and "parallelism" is that Hebrew employs a variety of devices to elevate its style, only one of which is parallelism. The choice of older terms, picturesque imagery, word plays, merism, inclusio, and terseness are all examples of heightened style which do not require the use of parallelism—and each of these styles can be present or absent in both poetry and prose. The bottom line is that the biblical authors were not bound by a set of rules about the kind of language and structure that could or could not be used in a given genre, as English writers are today.

It may be noted that biblical Hebrew has no words for "poetry" and "prose": these are Greek concepts, not Hebrew ones.[29] Further, the Greeks defined poetic structure on the basis of meter (sometimes rhyme as well), while Hebrew songs are non-metrical[30] and do not have rhyme. The Greek

---

[24] Kugel, *The Idea of Biblical Poetry*, 311.

[25] Ibid., 286.

[26] Ibid., 59-68.

[27] Ibid., 70.

[28] Ibid., 76-77.

[29] Ibid., 69-70, 127, 171-72.

[30] Bullock affirms that Hebrew poetry has a "rhythmic quality," but says "there is presently no scholarly consensus on the prominence of strict meter in Hebrew poetry" (C. Hassell Bullock, *An Introduction to the Old Testament Poetic Books* [Chicago: Moody Press, 1988], 32). However, Kugel has shown that there is no metrical system at all in Hebrew poetry, apart from "a loose and approximate regularity" in certain sections of the Bible (*Idea*

concept of poetry is therefore nonexistent in the Hebrew OT. Since the English concepts of poetry and prose are borrowed from the Greek concepts, one would have to redefine these terms to make them fit the pattern of writing in the OT; yet it is hard to see how such a redefinition would be helpful, or how the terms could be redefined in such a way that the Greco-English conception of poetry is not read back into the Hebrew one.

On the other hand, there are obvious differences between the writing styles of various texts in the Bible, and one ought to have some way to classify texts that are different. One idea is to classify genre solely by means of biblical terminology, such as proverb (מָשָׁל), song (שִׁיר), psalm (מִזמוֹר), law (תּוֹרָה), chronicle (סֵפֶר דִּבְרֵי הַיָּמִים), oracle (מַשָׂא), etc. These terms express the Hebrews' own conception of their form of writing, and do not impose our concepts of "poetry" and "prose" on the biblical text. Or, if one wishes to bifurcate the writing style of the OT in some way, it may be fair to speak of "narrative" and "non-narrative" texts, recognizing that a wide variety of styles still exists in each. But the explanation for many of the differences between narrative and non-narrative lies in a difference in subject matter, and not primarily in intentional structural differences. Again, the classification of OT writing into "poetry" and "prose" is not just a matter of semantics, for if one's understanding of "rules" for a given genre of Scripture is narrower than the author's own understanding of that writing style, the commentator may structure and interpret the text differently than the author intended—and, indeed, differently than the text itself permits.

Modern scholarship has become very enamored with the distinction between prose and poetry in the OT, and Kugel notes that over the past century an increasing number of texts have been marked as poetry.[31] Just looking at the English versions is telling: a 1901 ASV Bible only marks large sections of poetry in Job, Psalms, Proverbs, Song of Songs, and Lamentations, whereas newer English Bibles will mark about half of the OT as poetry. Today, mainly only narrative sections of Scripture—sections that are intended to tell a story—are marked as prose, and everything else is considered poetry. Even portions of narratives, such as curses and speeches, are now marked as poetry. Kugel notes two problems: first, many of these texts—especially in the prophetic books—exhibit intermittent or inconsistent parallelism, whereas the decision to mark them as poetry forces a parallelistic structure over the entire text.[32] Second, if one so wished, he could divide the entire OT into poetic lines and cola, showing that this has become more of a subjective than an objective exercise.[33] It is an exegetical fallacy to impose a "poetic" literary structure on a text that is generally not structured that way. Parallelism is really just a characteristic of elevated Hebrew style, and can be present—or lacking—in any genre of Scripture.

The term "parallelism" itself could be wrongly taken to imply synonymous meanings. Actually, the second line typically supports the first line, "carries it further, backs it up, completes it, goes beyond it."[34]

---

*of Biblical Poetry*, 301). In my own reading of Hebrew "poetry," I have found nothing approximating a fixed metrical system of the kind found in English songs and poetry. The complete lack of rhyme and meter in the Psalms has obvious practical implications: it implies that rhythm was not emphasized in temple music, and that there was no beat. It is not insignificant that drums are never mentioned in the Bible, even though they were used in surrounding cultures.

Interestingly, Foley calls the earliest Greek/Latin Christian songs "hymnodic psalmody" because they were imitative of the writing style of the OT Psalter, being quite unmetrical. The earliest example of metrical hymnody, i.e., songs that were written in a meter imitative of Greek poetry, comes from Clement of Alexandria early in the third century (Edward Foley, *Foundations of Christian Music: The Music of Pre-Constantinian Christianity* [Grove Books, 1992], 75-79).

[31] Kugel, *The Idea of Biblical Poetry*, 81.

[32] Even within the Psalter, Pss 23 and 137 lack clearly defined poetic lines, with parallel and balanced cola.

[33] Ibid., 82.

"The parallelistic style in the Bible consists not of stringing together clauses that bear some semantic, syntactic, or phonetic resemblance, nor yet of 'saying the same thing twice,' but of the sequence _____ / _____ // in which B is a continuation of A and yet broken from it by a pause, a typically emphatic, 'seconding' style in which parallelism plays an important part but whose essence is not parallelism, but the 'seconding sequence.'"[35] "All parallelism is really 'synthetic': it consists of A, a pause, and A's continuation B (or B + C)."[36] The second colon is the completion of the first: "A, and what's more, B"; "A, and as a matter of fact, B."[37] "Repetitions have been invented and reinvented a thousand times in the songs and poems of every people, prized not for their usefulness in the specific requirements of parallelistic style, but for the sense of return and completion on which every poetry thrives."[38] Repetition makes the reader pause and ponder what was previously said, yet also moves the thought of the first statement forward to some new idea or implication or image.

It seems that the rush to mark most of the OT as poetry is based on two factors: the popularity of literary criticism, and the rejection of the Bible as a supernatural revelation of inspired truth. The idea of "poetry" is key to interpreting the Bible as literature, since it is harder to justify the imposition of complex literary structures onto a prose text. The literary reading of the Bible is based on the premise that the Bible is a work of fiction that should be read as such, not a record of truth which must be read as fact rather than art. The literary interpretation of the Bible also seems to imply that it is no different from the literature of the surrounding cultures, and may be analyzed and viewed in the same way. It often views the Bible as a myth, like the epics of the pagans. As Bible believing Christians, the best way to take the text seriously is to look at what it actually says, and not to base our analysis of it on literary structure and background material. Kugel's remarks are incisive:

> One does not read the U.S. Constitution as literature, or *The Pageant of American History* as literature, or (to stick to an American context) Jonathan Edwards's sermons, *Poor Richard's Almanac*, or the Federal Reserve's *Monthly Bulletin* as literature. Respectively the legal, historical, sermonic, wisdom, and oracular genres surely account for the bulk of the twenty-four books of the Hebrew canon, and so one might well ask: what is literary about the Bible at all? Certainly it does not identify itself as literature, and often such self-definition as does occur seems clearly to place it elsewhere: "The word of the Lord came to me . . ." "Listen to my prayer . . ." "These are the generations . . ." "This is the regulation concerning . . ." "Hear, my son, your father's teaching"— all suppose a relationship between speaker and hearer which, we somehow feel, is double-crossed by being looked at *as* literature, as artful composition, as anything more than a faithful and naive recording. Of course we know better. Any text—that aforementioned U.S. Constitution, the warranty that comes with the clock-radio—can be opened and examined, its majestic or perhaps humble little strategies laid bare. Yet in this act the potential for inappropriateness, indeed absurdity, is high: in discovering alliteration here, or rhythmic patterns, we may truly find some of the unconscious or semiconscious "tinkerings of authorship," but we will seem to imply about the nature of the text and how it was written something that we actually believe to be untrue, or at least irrelevant. So with the Bible. We have shuddered to hear Joseph called "one of the most believable characters in Western literature," and not just because this statement puts the Bible on the wrong bookshelf. At such a remark one wants to object—on the model of the vaudevillian's "Who was that lady I saw you with last night?" "That ain't no lady, that's my wife"—and say that

---

[34] Ibid., 52.

[35] Ibid., 53-54.

[36] Ibid., 58

[37] Ibid., 42.

[38] Ibid., 39.

Joseph is no *character* at all, but someone far more intimately ours. And as true as this may be for us, how much truer must it have been when his story was first set down? That initial narrative act, "Come gather round and let me spin a tale," is not the starting point of biblical history. Its premise—"Let me tell you what happened to Joseph-our-ancestor, let me tell you how things came to be as you know them actually to be now"—is significantly different. Not to speak of "Let me tell you how God has saved us," "Let me tell you of God's teachings."[39]

Kugel's evaluation of the idea of Hebrew poetry is right. Though what has been said about characteristics of poetry accurately describes many verses (specifically) and texts (broadly), it is wrong to bifurcate Hebrew style into "poetry" and "prose." Most texts contain some elements of both styles. I would go beyond Kugel and claim that the word "poetry" cannot accurately describe any part of the Old Testament, with the possible exception of alphabetic acrostics.[40] Poetry follows a set of rules, but Hebrew "poetry" is not bound by strict or inviolable rules. Crucially, it lacks meter and rhyme. It may also be a disservice to visually divide "poetic" texts into colons, especially where such divisions are not readily apparent or where it is not clear that the text was meant to be sung or divided into pithy statements. If parallelism is clearly a feature of the text, the reader ought to be able to recognize it on his own. Paragraph divisions are preferable to line and colon divisions. Scholars have made too sharp of a distinction between poetry and prose, and have read too much into the significance of poetic structure. The structure of OT texts considered to be poetry is far too loose and too varied to fit them into a single category. Generalizations can be made, and patterns recognized, but each text must be analyzed on its own. Rather than speaking of poetry and prose, it is better to speak of narrative and non-narrative sections. Narrative is generally much easier to read because the vocabulary is more common, and the syntax more consistent.

Some people are convinced that parts of the OT are poetry simply because the Hebrew is much different than in what they call prose. However, the Greek of Mark is far different in vocabulary and word order than the Greek of Hebrews, yet no one would suggest that this makes Hebrews poetic. Also, Brian Webster and others have argued that what is called Hebrew poetry is actually quite close in word order and use of verb tenses to everyday Hebrew speech, and that it is actually Hebrew narrative which is the non-normative genre. The Psalms have more picturesque imagery than narrative, but this is because of their subject matter and devotional use, more than their literary structure.

There are very practical implications of the whole discussion of Hebrew poetry. In English, poems are usually not very serious or historical, and they often have an allegorical meaning. When scholars want to write something that communicates serious propositional truth, they write in prose. Thus, calling large sections of the OT "poetry" can imply that it is not intended to be taken seriously, thereby degrading the truth value of the text. This is done, for example, with Isaiah 40–66, in which many paragraphs in those chapters are marked as "songs" or "poems" in modern Bibles, though there is no evidence that they were in fact ever sung. This is sometimes done in the NT as well, by labeling key doctrinal sections as early Christian hymnology. Also, in English, poetry is often highly figurative. Thus, when parts of the Bible are labeled as "poetry," this can be used as an excuse to disregard the literal sense of the text, as in Genesis 1. There are, of course, portions of the OT that use more figures of speech than others, but these have always been recognized by interpreters through the use of common sense. In the end, the discussion of Hebrew "poetry" within the context of the literary reading of Scripture is unhelpful and should be discarded.

---

[39] Kugel, *Idea of Biblical Poetry*, 303-4.

[40] There is, in some contexts, a difference between saying that a text is "poetic" and saying it is "poetry." Someone can use poetic (i.e., elevated or picturesque) language in a prose speech.

## The Music of Ancient Israel

The Holy Spirit did not see fit to record in Scripture the tunes to which the psalms were sung, or musical scores for the temple orchestra. It is easy to see why God did not want these tunes recorded—later generations would view them as the only acceptable tunes to which the psalms may be sung, or even as the only acceptable tunes in all the world. There probably was no musical notation in existence at the time the Psalter was written, though one could have been created if it were thought to be necessary. However, the musical instruments in use at the time were greatly limited in range and expression, and the simple melodies could easily be passed from one performer to another. The melodies were probably not viewed as fixed, either, but could be modified by the performer as he desired—a practice which is well documented in the early church and was probably taken over from Judaism. "In the first Christian churches and up to about the eighth century the singing of the chants was *improvisatory*: not, of course, 'free' spontaneous improvisation, but performance in which traditional melodic structures or 'melody-types' associated with particular parts of the liturgy or particular seasons of the church year furnished a basis on which the singer embroidered, making use also of certain standard melodic formulas in the course of his improvisation."[41]

Certain psalms are specifically noted as having been set to specific melodies. Although translations are disputed, the following are found in the ASV:

- Sheminith—Pss 6, 12
- Muth-labben—Ps 9
- Aijeleth hash-Shahar—Ps 22
- Shoshannim—Pss 45, 69
- Alamoth—Ps 46
- Mahalath—Ps 53
- Jonath elem rehokim—Ps 56
- Al-tash-heth—Pss 57–59, 75
- Shushan Eduth—Ps 60
- Shoshannim Eduth—Ps 80
- Gittith—Pss 81, 84
- Mahalath Leannoth—Ps 88

It is known that in ancient Jewish music, as well as in its continuation in the early church, a single melody-type could be adapted, by the use of slight variations, to accommodate any given text.[42] Such music was written in what we would call "chant" style, i.e., without any metrical pattern (among other features).

A number of musical instruments are named in the psalter, as well as in other places in the OT. These included woodwinds and plucked stringed instruments to provide melody, while trumpets and percussion (not drums) provided fanfare.[43] While in most instances we have a good general idea of what

---

[41] Donald Jay Grout, *A History of Western Music* (rev. ed.; New York: W. W. Norton, 1973), 43.

[42] See Grout, *A History of Western Music*, 46.

[43] Most modern lexicons, commentaries, and reference works seem to assume that the Israelites had and used drums, and even include the word "drums" in their Bible translations. Older works do exactly the opposite—they assume that the Israelites neither had nor used drums, and the word "drum" does not appear in any older Bible translation. The reason for the difference is that it is inconceivable to a believer that drums would have been used in temple worship, while it is equally inconceivable to unbelievers that they would not have been. In point of fact, there is no Hebrew word in the OT that either can or must properly be translated as "drum" (outside, possibly, of the

these instruments were, images of them are virtually nonexistent. Without seeing, hearing, and handling one of the actual instruments, it is difficult to tell exactly what it sounded like and how it was played. Again, it is possible to form a general idea, but details are mere guesswork.

The Davidic choir was well organized, and consisted of a large number of paid, professional, full-time musicians and singers. These musicians and singers were members of Israel's clergy, specially ordained priests and Levites.

### Overview of the Psalms

The following section provides a brief overview of each of the psalms, including a statement of the subject and author, and an outline. For selected Psalms, a more extensive discussion of interpretive issues is also included.

---

*Book I – Psalms 1–41 – Psalms of David (Personal Emphasis)*

---

# Psalm 1

**Subject:** The enduring prosperity of the righteous contrasted with the speedy ruin of the wicked
**Author:** Not stated, but almost certainly David

**Outline**
  I.  The blessings of the righteous vv. 1-3
 II.  The ruin of the wicked vv. 4-5
III.  Summary statement v. 6

Psalms 1 and 2 are both big-picture psalms, and were intentionally placed at the front of the Psalter for this reason. Psalm 1 teaches that as we go through life we must make a choice to follow God's Word in order to receive blessing. Psalm 2, which is about Jesus Christ, teaches how it will all turn out.

---

# Psalm 2

**Subject:**  The rule of the Messiah over the nations
**Author:** No superscription, but Acts 4:25 attributes to David

**Outline**
  I.  Vision of Armageddon vv. 1-9
      A. The position and attitude of the nations vv. 1-3
      B. The position and attitude of God vv. 4-6
      C. The position and attitude of the Messiah vv. 7-9
 II.  Earth's rulers admonished by the Psalmist vv. 10-12

---

Aramaic list of Nebuchadnezzar's instruments in Dan 3), and it should be obvious to any believer that drums would not have been approved by God for use in His worship.

Verses one through nine of this psalm consist of a far-reaching vision in which David sees the end of human history (in vv. 1-3), the scene in the heavenly courts at that time (in vv. 4-6), and the Messiah entering upon universal dominion (in vv. 7-9). In the final three verses (vv. 10-12), David remonstrates with the kings of the earth in any age, counseling them to honor Yahweh and His Son now, before it is too late, and they are utterly broken along with the other rulers of the earth.

Reasons for a strictly messianic interpretation of Psalm 2:
- This psalm is adduced by the writer of Hebrews (1:5) as a proof of Christ's divinity—something which it could not be if the psalm originally found application to a mere human ruler.
- This psalm is quoted frequently in the New Testament, and each time it is specifically applied to Jesus Christ, not to a historical situation in Israel.
- No historical Davidic king is said to have ruled the nations with a rod of iron (v. 9), but Christ is said to do so three times in the book of Revelation (2:27; 12:5; 19:15).
- There is only one Son in the psalm (v. 7, "my son"), and He is given universal and absolute dominion (vv. 8-9). All men are required to honor the Son and to do Him homage (v. 12). When this Son becomes angry, the nations will perish (v. 12), whereas the same could not be said of any human king. Finally, those who take refuge in Him are called "blessed" or "happy" (v. 12), while in another psalm it is said that those who hope in Yahweh are happy (Ps 146:5). Since those who put their trust in princes and in men are rebuked (Ps 146:3-4; cf. Jer 17:5-7), this Son cannot be a mere man.
- The King in this psalm is once called the "Messiah," the Anointed One (v. 2), and He is twice called the Son of God (vv. 7, 12).
- If the language of this psalm is taken literally, it cannot apply to any Davidic king but the Messiah.

---

# Psalm 3

**Subject:** A prayer of trust in God in the midst of danger
**Author:** David

**Outline**
I. The present distress vv. 1-2
II. Yahweh the source of help and protection vv. 3-4
III. Confidence in the midst of danger vv. 5-6
IV. Prayer for deliverance and blessing vv. 7-8

---

# Psalm 4

**Subject:** A prayer of trust in God after the passing of immediate danger
**Author:** David

**Outline**
I. Appeal to God v. 1
II. Remonstrance with enemies vv. 2-5
III. The supreme joy of perfect trust vv. 6-8

# Psalm 5

**Subject:** A prayer for protection from wicked enemies
**Author:** David

**Outline**
  I.   David's cry to God vv. 1-3
  II.  God's intolerance of the wicked and acceptance of the righteous vv. 4-7
  III. Prayer for personal deliverance and the destruction of David's enemies vv. 8-12

# Psalm 6

**Subject:** A prayer for mercy in a time of trouble
**Author:** David

**Outline**
  I.  Cry for relief in suffering vv. 1-7
  II. Confidence in deliverance and vindication vv. 8-10

The setting for this psalm is often assumed to be a serious sin committed by David, and thus it has been classified as a penitential psalm. However, sin is never mentioned in this psalm; David never confesses his sin or expresses repentance and asks forgiveness. Rather, in v. 7, David says he is grieved because of his adversaries. The reference to David's bones being troubled in v. 2, and his prayer for healing in the same verse, indicate that he was suffering a severe and protracted physical illness. This is also indicated in vv. 5-7, which speak of his nearness to death and his physical anguish at night. The severity and length of this illness had created an occasion for David's enemies to reproach him and to claim that he was forsaken by Yahweh (vv. 7-10). Psalm 22 describes a very similar circumstance. The primary reason that many commentators think David had sinned is his prayer for relief from God's affliction of him (v. 1). However, the ancient Israelites recognized that God is responsible for all natural events, and therefore if a person was ill, it was God who sent the illness (cf. Ruth 1:21). God often afflicts His children for reasons that have nothing to do with sin. Note that the words used for chastening in v. 1 do not always refer to discipline for sin.

# Psalm 7

**Subject:** Yahweh implored to defend David against the wicked
**Author:** David

**Outline**
  I.  David's prayer for divine intervention vv. 1-10
      A. The urgency of David's need vv. 1-2
      B. David's innocence vv. 3-5
      C. Prayer for God's judgment vv. 6-8
      D. Prayer for the triumph of the righteous vv. 9-10
  II. The judgment of the wicked vv. 11-17
      A. God's execution of vengeance on the wicked vv. 11-13

    B. The self-destructiveness of wicked behavior vv. 14-16
    C. David's praise for the manifestation of God's righteousness v. 17

# Psalm 8

**Subject:** David praises God for His choice of man as His ruling representative on earth
**Author:** David

**Outline**
   I. God's exalted status vv. 1-3
  II. Man's elevated status vv. 4-8
III. God's honor through man v. 9

    God's original intent for man is ultimately realized in the Person and work of the Messiah. Although this psalm is not a messianic prophecy, it has messianic implications, since the Messiah fulfills God's ideal for man (cf. Heb 2:5-18).

# Psalm 9

**Subject:** Yahweh praised for His deliverance of the righteous from godless nations, and implored to deliver them again
**Author:** David

**Outline**
    I. Thanksgiving for Yahweh's judgment of David's enemies vv. 1-6
   II. Yahweh glorified for His righteous rule vv. 7-12
 III. Prayer for mercy and deliverance vv. 13-14
 IV. Anticipation of deliverance vv. 15-16
  V. The surety of the Yahweh's vengeance on the nations vv. 17-18
 VI. Prayer for Yahweh's judgment of the nations vv. 19-20

    Psalms 9 and 10 are closely linked, and present many difficulties and complex literary problems for the exegete. These two psalms are also among the most difficult in the Psalter to translate; English translations read easily by necessity, but the underlying Hebrew does not.[44]
    Psalms 9 and 10 together form an unusual broken acrostic, in which almost every other line begins with a consecutive letter of the Hebrew alphabet, but with some irregularities.[45] Psalm 10 skips out of the

---

[44] That the language is highly poetic is shown by the five occurrences of the negative adverb בַּל in Ps 10, an unusual concentration.

[45] Following the Hebrew verse numeration, 9:8 seems like it should begin with דּ or הּ, but instead it appears that both letters are skipped (unless emendations are followed), and 9:8-11 all begin with ו instead. 9:19 begins with כּ, when 9:20 would have to begin with this letter to fit the pattern of an every-other-verse acrostic (unless one considers כּ to be represented by ק in 9:20). There are six letters skipped in 10:2-11 (מ, נ, ס, ע, פ, צ), although this section contains the proper number of cola to contain them.

acrostic in vv. 3-11 (the description of the wicked man) before rejoining it for the final four letters. Still, enough of the letters are present to consider the acrostic as legitimate, and not a mere coincidence or scholarly contrivance.

Although Psalms 9 and 10 are combined in the LXX, they were probably not so originally, for it is highly unlikely that Hebrew manuscripts would divide these psalms in two if they were originally a single composition—with an acrostic structure and no superscription on Ps 10, no less. The tendency would be to combine these psalms, not to separate them. Also, Ps 9:20 sounds like a conclusion, while Ps 10:1 sounds like the beginning of a new composition. However, although these are two independent psalms, they were probably composed together, with the tenth Psalm written to complement the ninth.

Psalms 9 and 10 are similar in language and structure, but distinct in tone and subject matter. Linguistic similarities include the unique expression לְעִתּוֹת בַּצָּרָה (*in times of trouble*, 9:9; 10:1), the rare term דַּךְ (*oppressed*, 9:9; 10:18), the rare term אֱנוֹשׁ for "man" at the close of each psalm (9:19-20; 10:18), "for ever and ever" (9:5; 10:16), "Arise, O Yahweh" (9:19; 10:12), and others. However, while in Ps 9 the writer frequently refers to himself in the first person, in Ps 10 he never does. Kirkpatrick notes other differences in tone and subject as follows:

> Ps. ix is a triumphant thanksgiving, rarely passing into prayer (*vv.* 13, 19): its theme is the manifestation of God's sovereign righteousness in the defeat and destruction of *foreign enemies* of the nation. Ps. x is a plaintive expostulation and prayer, describing the tyrannous conduct of *godless men within the nation*, and pleading that God will no longer delay to vindicate His righteousness, and prove Himself the Defender of the helpless.
>
> . . . .
>
> Ps. ix however appears to be complete in itself, and it seems preferable to regard Ps. x as a companion piece rather than as part of a continuous whole.
>
> The connexion of thought is clear. The Psalmist has watched the great conflict between good and evil being waged in two fields: in the world, between Israel and the heathen nations; in the nation of Israel, between godless oppressors of the weak and their innocent victims. He has seen the sovereignty of God decisively vindicated in the world by the defeat of Israel's enemies: but when he surveys the conflict within the nation, wrong seems to be triumphant. So he prays for an equally significant demonstration of God's sovereignty within the nation by a signal punishment of the wicked who deny His power or will to interpose.[46]

---

# Psalm 10

**Subject:** Plea for God to judge godless sinners who oppress the poor and deny the reality of judgment because of its delay

**Author:** Not stated, but David assumed from the previous psalm

**Outline**

I.   Remonstrance with God for His delay in judging the wicked vv. 1-2
II.  The wicked man's fearless commission of evil vv. 3-11
III. Call for God to judge vv. 12-15
IV.  Confident expectation of God's judgment of the wicked vv. 16-18

---

[46] Kirkpatrick, *Psalms*, 41-42.

# Psalm 11

**Subject:** An expression of confidence in God in response to the threats of the wicked
**Author:** David

**Outline**
   I.  The admonition to flee rejected vv. 1-3
  II.  God's response to men's actions vv. 4-7

---

# Psalm 12

**Subject:** God entreated to help the righteous in a wicked age
**Author:** David

**Outline**
   I.  The plight of the righteous while faithlessness prevails vv. 1-2
      A. The cry for help and its reason v. 1
      B. Their faithlessness described v. 2
  II.  The judgment of the boastful vv. 3-4
 III.  The preservation of the righteous vv. 5-7
 IV.  The cause of the wicked age observed v. 8

---

# Psalm 13

**Subject:** Prayer for deliverance as David's enemies press upon him
**Author:** David

**Outline**
   I.  Complaint in distress vv. 1-2
  II.  Appeal for deliverance before it is too late vv. 3-4
 III.  Joy in hope of deliverance vv. 5-6

---

# Psalm 14

**Subject:** The corruption of man is described, then illustrated in man's oppression of God's people and the punishment they receive for it. The psalm ends with a prayer for full deliverance.
**Author:** David

**Outline**
   I.  The universal depravity of man vv. 1-3
  II.  Persecution of God's people v. 4
 III.  God's defense of His people vv. 5-6
 IV.  Prayer for full deliverance v. 7

This psalm is almost identical with Psalm 53. Verses 5-6 are the major difference.

# Psalm 15

**Subject:** Description of the man who will dwell with God
**Author:** David

**Outline**
 I. The subject introduced v. 1
 II. Characteristics of the man who will dwell with God vv. 2-5b
III. Conclusion v. 5c

This psalm is a tremendous description of a righteous, godly man.

# Psalm 16

**Subject:** A description of David's commitment to Yahweh and Yahweh's blessings of him. A messianic Psalm, probably best viewed as typological.
**Author:** David

**Outline**
 I. Prayer for preservation on the grounds of commitment to Yahweh vv. 1-4
 II. Yahweh his sole good and source of good vv. 5-8
III. The joy and benefits of his relationship with Yahweh vv. 9-11

Peter's interpretation of this psalm in Acts 2 is almost certainly taken directly from Jesus' teaching concerning Himself (Luke 24:44-47).

# Psalm 17

**Subject:** A prayer for deliverance from oppressors
**Author:** David

**Outline**
 I. Appeal for justice on the ground of personal integrity vv. 1-5
 II. Appeal for deliverance on the ground of personal relationship vv. 5-9
III. The wickedness and deadliness of his enemies vv. 10-12
IV. Appeal for just recompense vv. 13-15

# Psalm 18

**Subject:** A hymn of thanksgiving for Yahweh's lifelong deliverance and exaltation of David
**Author:** David

**Outline**

I. Yahweh's protection of David vv. 1-3
II. Yahweh's deliverance of David from great distress vv. 4-19
   A. David's distress and cry vv. 4-6
   B. Yahweh's power manifested vv. 7-15
   C. Yahweh's deliverance vv. 16-19
III. Yahweh's faithfulness to the righteous vv. 20-29
   A. David's integrity vv. 20-23
   B. Yahweh's dealings with the wicked and the righteous vv. 24-27
   C. Yahweh's all-sufficiency to David vv. 28-29
IV. David's defeat of his enemies through Yahweh vv. 30-42
V. Yahweh's exaltation of David vv. 43-45
VI. David's blessing and praise of Yahweh vv. 46-50

This psalm is almost exactly duplicated in 2 Samuel 22.

# Psalm 19

**Subject:** A celebration of general and special revelation, concluded by a prayer for uprightness
**Author:** David

**Outline**

I. General revelation vv. 1-6
II. Special revelation vv. 7-11
III. Prayer for uprightness vv. 12-14

# Psalm 20

**Subject:** A liturgical prayer for victory in battle
**Author:** David

**Outline**

I. The people's intercession for the king vv. 1-5
II. The king's anticipation of victory vv. 6-8
III. Concluding prayer spoken by all v. 9

# Psalm 21

**Subject:** A liturgical prayer of thanksgiving for the king's victory in battle
**Author:** David

**Outline**

I. Thanksgiving for the king's victory through Yahweh vv. 1-7
II. Anticipation of the king's future triumphs vv. 8-12
III. Concluding congregational prayer v. 13

This is a companion Psalm to the previous one, to be sung after success in battle.

# Psalm 22

**Subject:** A prayer for deliverance in the midst of extreme anguish, followed by praise for answered prayer. A typological messianic psalm.
**Author:** David

**Outline**
I. David's prayer for deliverance vv. 1-21
   A. David's cry to God vv. 1-2
   B. God's past deliverance of others vv. 3-5
   C. David's degraded state vv. 6-8
   D. David's closeness to God vv. 9-11
   E. David's assailants vv. 12-13
   F. David's anguish vv. 14-15
   G. David's affliction by his assailants vv. 16-18
   H. David's plea for deliverance vv. 19-21a
   I. The prayer answered v. 21b
II. Praise for answered prayer vv. 22-31
   A. David's personal thanksgiving vv. 22-26
   B. The worship of others vv. 26-31

# Psalm 23

**Subject:** David praises Yahweh as his shepherd and host
**Author:** David

**Outline**
I. Yahweh as David's shepherd vv. 1-4
II. Yahweh as David's host vv. 5-6

This psalm is often misread to be centered around the theme "Yahweh is my shepherd." In reality, this theme is only present in the first four verses. Verses 5-6 are not about sheep and shepherds, but are about men and God. Verses 5-6 apply the general image of vv. 1-4 to the specific situation of the Psalmist, and show that God is more than a need-meeter—He is my host/friend/intimate companion. There is thus movement in this psalm towards a climax.

# Psalm 24

**Subject:** Zion summons Yahweh to enter its gates following an exaltation of Yahweh's majesty and a restriction on those allowed access to Yahweh's sanctuary.
**Author:** David

**Outline**
I. Yahweh's universal dominion vv. 1-2
II. Conditions for access to Yahweh's sanctuary vv. 3-6
III. Zion summoned to admit its true King vv. 7-10

Kirkpatrick argues convincingly that this beautiful psalm was composed on the occasion when David brought the ark of the covenant into Jerusalem from the house of Obed-edom.

# Psalm 25

**Subject:** Prayer for deliverance, defense, pardon, guidance, and blessing
**Author:** David

**Outline**
I. Prayer for protection, guidance, and pardon vv. 1-7
II. Praise for Yahweh's manner of dealing with the upright vv. 8-14
III. Prayer for deliverance in distress vv. 15-22

Psalms 25 and 34 are also acrostic in form, with each line beginning with a successive letter of the Hebrew alphabet. Both of these psalms skip the letter *wāw*, though in Psalm 25 a *wāw* is inserted at the beginning of the final colon of the *hē* line by the LXX, Syriac, and a few Hebrew MSS, perhaps in a misguided attempt to "correct" the MT by inserting a *wāw* line. *BHS* further suggests transferring part of v. 7 to v. 5 to complete the line. However, an analysis of these Psalms shows that the *wāw* line was intentionally skipped to form a double acrostic. Skipping the *wāw* creates an odd number of letters in the alphabet (twenty-one), which puts *lāmed* exactly in the middle. Psalms 25 and 34 both add a *pe* line after *tāw* (at the end), to keep the number of lines at twenty-two. When this additional *pe* is taken together with the first and middle letters of the acrostic ('*ālep* and *lāmed*), the letters spell '*ālep*, the first letter of the alphabet. Most likely, *wāw* was the letter chosen to be omitted because there is only one word beginning with *wāw* that could be used in an acrostic. Attempts to "correct" the "omission" of the *wāw* line actually ruin the poetic structure of these psalms. Psalm 25 also has the peculiar trait of having two *rêš* lines (rather than *qôp – rêš*). Many reasons for this have been suggested, but it is possibly because David felt that there was no appropriate way to form a *qôp* line.

# Psalm 26

**Subject:** David protests his integrity and prays for deliverance from the fate of the wicked
**Author:** David

**Outline**
I. David's plea for the recognition of his integrity vv. 1-3
II. The proof of David's integrity vv. 4-7
III. Prayer to share in the fate of the righteous, not sinners vv. 8-12

# Psalm 27

**Subject:** An expression of confident trust in Yahweh, followed by a prayer for protection from adversaries
**Author:** David

**Outline**
  I. Fearless trust and rest in God vv. 1-6
  II. Prayer for protection from adversaries vv. 7-14

---

# Psalm 28

**Subject:** Prayer for deliverance and retribution followed by thanksgiving for answered prayer
**Author:** David

**Outline**
  I. Prayer for deliverance and retribution vv. 1-5
  II. Thanksgiving for answered prayer vv. 6-9

---

# Psalm 29

**Subject:** A psalm exalting the greatness and power of Yahweh
**Author:** David

**Outline**
  I. Angels summoned to worship Yahweh vv. 1-2
  II. Yahweh's majesty revealed on earth vv. 3-9
  III. Yahweh's eternal rule vv. 10-11

---

# Psalm 30

**Subject:** Thanksgiving for deliverance from death in answer to prayer
**Author:** David

**Outline**
  I. Thanksgiving for deliverance from death vv. 1-3
  II. An invitation to join in thanksgiving vv. 4-5
  III. David's presumption and God's chastisement vv. 6-7
  IV. David's plea for his life to be spared vv. 8-10
  V. The answer to prayer and its purpose vv. 11-12

---

# Psalm 31

**Subject:** David earnestly prays for deliverance in the midst of serious attacks by his enemies, then praises Yahweh when his prayer is answered
**Author:** David

**Outline**

I. Prayer for deliverance from adversaries vv. 1-18
II. Praise of Yahweh for answered prayer vv. 19-24

# Psalm 32

**Subject:** The blessedness of forgiveness and of trust in God
**Author:** David

**Outline**

I. The blessedness of forgiveness vv. 1-2
II. The burden of guilt vv. 3-4
III. Pardon through prayer vv. 5-6
IV. The Psalmist's trust in Yahweh and its rewards vv. 7-8
V. Lot of the godly and wicked contrasted vv. 9-10
VI. Exhortation for the righteous to rejoice in God v. 11

This psalm was probably a reflection on David's sin with Bathsheba, which was followed by a period of guilt, then confession, then restoration.

# Psalm 33

**Subject:** An exhortation to praise and trust Yahweh, with a list of reasons why Yahweh is praiseworthy and trustworthy
**Author:** No superscription, but must be Davidic because of its placement in Book I

**Outline**

I. Call to praise v. 1-3
II. Reasons to praise and trust Yahweh vv. 4-19
   A. His moral attributes vv. 4-5
   B. His creation of all things vv. 6-7
   C. His omnipotence vv. 8-9
   D. His sovereign rule vv. 10-11
   E. His choice of His people v. 12
   F. Yahweh's omniscience vv. 13-15
   G. The weakness of earthly powers vv. 16-17
   H. Yahweh's faithfulness to His servants vv. 18-19
III. Profession of trust in Yahweh vv. 20-22

This psalm is probably placed after the previous one because its first verse is similar to the last verse of Psalm 32. Some have suggested that because Psalm 33 lacks a superscription, it was originally joined to Psalm 32, but this does not seem likely on the basis of manuscript evidence.

# Psalm 34

**Subject:** A psalm of praise to Yahweh for his care for the righteous
**Author:** David

**Outline**
  I. Celebration of Yahweh's care for those who fear Him vv. 1-10
 II. Exhortation to fear Yahweh vv. 11-14
III. Description of Yahweh's care for the righteous vv. 15-22

Psalm 34 is an alphabetic acrostic, with each line beginning with a successive letter of the Hebrew alphabet (with two exceptions). See comments on Psalm 25.

# Psalm 35

**Subject:** An imprecatory prayer for vengeance upon David's enemies
**Author:** David

**Outline**
  I. Prayer for destruction of David's enemies vv. 1-10
 II. The greatness of the injustice against David vv. 11-16
III. Prayer to be rescued and vindicated vv. 17-28

Each of the three major divisions of this psalm ends with a vow of thanksgiving.

# Psalm 36

**Subject:** The conduct of the godless man contrasted with the lovingkindness of Yahweh toward those who know Him
**Author:** David

**Outline**
  I. The conduct of the godless man vv. 1-4
 II. The beneficence of Yahweh toward the godly vv. 7-9
III. Prayer for blessing, protection, and retribution vv. 10-12

# Psalm 37

**Subject:** The insecurity of the wicked contrasted with the security of those who trust in Yahweh
**Author:** David

**Outline**

 I.   Counsel not to envy evildoers vv. 1-11
 II.  The shortlived prosperity of the wicked vv. 12-20
 III. The sure and abiding reward of the righteous vv. 21-31
 IV.  Summary: end of the righteous and wicked contrasted vv. 32-40

This is an acrostic psalm, in which every fourth colon (every other line) begins with a consecutive letter of the Hebrew alphabet. The acrostic in this psalm is unusual in that a particle precedes the word beginning with the acrostic letter in the lines for the ʻ*ayin* and *tāw*.

This psalm, like Psalm 73 and the book of Job, deals with the old problem of evil in the world—why do the wicked seem to prosper, while times are tough for the righteous? For the righteous man who is suffering persecution for his faithfulness to God, this is a very comforting psalm.

# Psalm 38

**Subject:** David pleads to be delivered from an illness that came to him as chastisement for sin
**Author:** David

**Outline**

 I.   The pains of chastisement vv. 1-8
 II.  External pressures vv. 9-14
 III. Pleadings for deliverance vv. 15-22

David was one of the greatest men of God who ever lived, and yet the Psalms reveal that he often struggled greatly with sin, and suffered chastisement for it. People who put on an air of perfection are false and hypocritical.

# Psalm 39

**Subject:** A prayerful reflection on the vanity of life after a crisis of suffering
**Author:** David

**Outline**

 I.   The resolution of silence vv. 1-2
 II.  The prayer to understand life's vanity vv. 3-6
 III. The prayer to be stayed upon God vv. 7-9
 IV.  The prayer for relief and respite vv. 10-13

The Psalm is apparently a sequel to the preceding one, a reflection on what had happened after the crisis has passed.

# Psalm 40

**Subject:** David prays for speedy deliverance in light of past blessings and public proclamation of Yahweh's faithfulness to the righteous
**Author:** David

**Outline**
  I.  Declaration of God's past faithfulness vv. 1-10
  II. Plea for present deliverance vv. 11-17

    Part of this psalm is messianic; vv. 6-8 are quoted in Hebrews 10:5-7.

---

# Psalm 41

**Subject:** A prayer for healing from a serious illness and deliverance from mocking enemies, bracketed
    by expressions of confidence in and praise for Yahweh's faithfulness
**Author:** David

**Outline**
  I.   David's confidence in Yahweh vv. 1-3
  II.  David's prayer for deliverance vv. 4-10
  III. David's praise for Yahweh's faithfulness vv. 11-13

---

*Book II – Psalms 42–72 – Psalms for the Chief Musician*

---

# Psalms 42–43

**Subject:** The prayer of a temple singer to return to Jerusalem to worship Yahweh after an attack by an
    enemy nation
**Author:** The sons of Korah; probably a single Korahite temple singer wrote both Ps 42 and Ps 43. The
    use of "God" rather than "Yahweh" is typical of the compositions of the sons of Korah, and
    atypical of Davidic Psalms. Psalms 42 and 43 were probably originally one psalm, and are
    joined together in many Hebrew manuscripts (thirty-seven of Kennicott and De Rossi). This
    composition is easily divided into three stanzas by the repetition of a refrain.

**Outline**
  I.   The yearning of the Psalmist's soul for God 42:1-5
  II.  The Psalmist's plight 42:6-11
  III. Prayer for deliverance 43:1-5

    The circumstances of writing are spelled out in 42:6. This temple singer has been forced to leave
Jerusalem and is north of the Sea of Galilee, in the upper Jordan region, where he is taunted by his
enemies. He remembers leading great liturgical celebrations at the feasts and longs to return to Jerusalem
to worship. Such a situation must have occurred before the split of the northern kingdom from the
southern kingdom, and the most likely historical background is the Edomite sneak attack on Jerusalem
during David's reign, while the main Israelite army was fighting Aram in the north.

---

# Psalm 44

**Subject:** In the aftermath of a lost battle, God's past deliverances are recalled and a plea is made for deliverance from the present distress
**Author:** One of the sons of Korah

**Outline**
  I.   God's past deliverances recalled vv. 1-8
 II.   The present distress vv. 9-16
III.   Israel's faithfulness protested vv. 17-22
IV.   The plea for deliverance vv. 23-26

This psalm was written after the Israelite army had suffered a serious defeat, with disastrous results (vv. 9-16). Probably this is the same assault which prompted the writing of Psalms 42–43.

# Psalm 45

**Subject:** A celebration of a king's marriage, probably Solomon's; a typological messianic psalm
**Author:** One of the sons of Korah

**Outline**
  I.   The king addressed and praised vv. 1-9
 II.   The bride addressed and celebrated vv. 10-15
III.   Celebration of the king's future posterity vv. 16-17

This psalm is about the goodness of the king. It is a hyperbolic description of Israel's most glorious king, using language which applies to the ultimate Son of David. The divine honors cannot be applied literally to Solomon, but they do apply literally to the Messiah. However, the language used in this psalm does legitimately apply to Solomon when understood metaphorically.

This is the only Psalm about marital love, or that is called a song of loves. The only other song in Scripture about love is the Song of Songs—and therefore we may surmise a connection between the marriage herein described and that described in Song of Songs. The occasion for writing is court poets who are celebrating the marriage of the king, and who take the opportunity to speak of the goodness of the king.

# Psalm 46

**Subject:** A celebration of God's presence in the midst of His city and people as the ground of their confidence in the past, present, and future
**Author:** The sons of Korah

**Outline**
  I.   God a refuge in the midst of turbulence vv. 1-3
 II.   God's presence is the joy and security of His people vv. 4-7
III.   The portent of God's final and absolute supremacy vv. 8-11

There is a close connection between Psalms 46, 47, and 48. All are songs of praise to God for the deliverance and protection of Zion from the nations after a time of war. Kirkpatrick thinks it virtually certain that the occasion for the composition of these Psalms was the deliverance of Jerusalem from Sennacherib in 701; however, there is no reason why they could not date to the reign of David.

# Psalm 47

**Subject:** A celebration of God's sovereignty over the nations, as illustrated by His defeat of Zion's enemies

**Author:** The sons of Korah

**Outline**
I. Summons to praise Yahweh in view of his choice of Israel vv. 1-4
II. Renewed summons to praise Yahweh as King vv. 5-7
III. Ultimate realization of God's sovereignty in the homage of the nations vv. 8-9

# Psalm 48

**Subject:** Celebration of the safety and sanctity of Zion as a result of God's presence

**Author:** The sons of Korah

**Outline**
I. The greatness of Yahweh and the glory of Zion vv. 1-2
II. Yahweh's defense of Zion vv. 3-8
III. Invitation to reflect on Zion and her God vv. 9-14

# Psalm 49

**Subject:** A didactic psalm which teaches the folly of trusting in riches and loving money

**Author:** The sons of Korah

**Outline**
I. Universal summons to listen vv. 1-4
II. The uselessness of wealth for preventing death vv. 5-12
III. The end of the wealthy wicked vv. 13-20

# Psalm 50

**Subject:** A didactic and prophetic psalm depicting a judgment scene at which God gives a report card to His people, including both saints and sinners

**Author:** Asaph

**Message:** Faith that is genuine must be accompanied by works; no one will be saved merely by profession or association, nor will any believer please God merely by performance of rituals.

**Outline**
  I.   The advent of God to judge His people vv. 1-6
  II.  God's judgment of Israel as a whole vv. 7-15
  III. God's judgment of shameless hypocrites vv. 16-21
  IV.  Epilogue of warning and promise vv. 22-23

Asaph was the chief musician, so it is natural that one of his psalms should be included in the book of psalms for the chief musician (Book II). Psalm 50 forms a hinge between the psalms of the sons of Korah (42–49) and the Davidic psalms in Book II (51–71), as described in the introduction. In its nearer context, Ps 50, describing God's judgment of His people, leads directly into David's confession of sin and plea for mercy in Ps 51. Likewise, the message of Ps 49, regarding the temporality of honor and money in this life, is related to the warning given to the complacent hypocrites in Ps 50. Although Pss 49 and 50 are both didactic, Ps 49 has more of a "wisdom" character, while Ps 50 has more of a prophetic character. In accordance with this distinction, all peoples are addressed in Ps 49, whereas only the people of God are addressed in Ps 50.

This unique psalm presents a most singular picture, full of profundity and beauty. Asaph, the writer of the psalm, sees an otherwise invisible judgment scene in a prophetic vision: Yahweh, the God of Israel, comes in majestic glory and calls His people to a great tribunal in which He will issue an evaluation of them (vv. 1-6). Addressing His people as a whole, God acknowledges that they are offering sacrifices faithfully, but declares that what He really wants is praise from a pure heart (vv. 7-15). God then identifies and rebukes hypocrites within the covenant community, who professed to be part of His people, but denied Him by their works (vv. 16-21). The psalm ends with a stern epilogue of warning and promise: God will assuredly judge those who disregard Him, but He will save those who glorify Him and order their ways in accordance with His statutes (vv. 22-23). The message of this psalm is that no one will be saved by a profession alone; faith that is genuine must be accompanied by works.

---

# Psalm 51

**Subject:** The prayer of a penitent sinner for pardon and restoration
**Author:** David

**Outline**
  I.    Plea for forgiveness and cleansing vv. 1-2
  II.   Confession of sin vv. 3-4
  III.  Natural corruption contrasted with true righteousness vv. 4-6
  IV.   Prayer for cleansing and restoration vv. 7-8
  V.    Prayer for forgiveness and inner cleansing vv. 9-10
  VI.   Prayer for spiritual restoration vv. 11-12
  VII.  Resolve to regain spiritual usefulness vv. 13-15
  VIII. The grounds for forgiveness vv. 16-17
  IX.   Prayer for restoration and blessing vv. 18-19

This psalm is probably one-of-a-kind for a powerful king in the ancient Near East. None of the pagan kings wished to admit wrongdoing or to humble himself and repent before God.

---

# Psalm 52

**Subject:** A didactic psalm, contrasting the futility of the wicked man's wickedness with the triumph of the righteous
**Author:** David

**Outline**
I. Remonstrance with the wicked man vv. 1-5
II. The triumph of the righteous vv. 6-9

# Psalm 53

**Subject:** The corruption of man is described, then illustrated in man's oppression of God's people and the punishment they receive for it. The psalm ends with a prayer for full deliverance.
**Author:** David

**Outline**
I. The universal depravity of man vv. 1-3
II. Persecution of God's people and its punishment vv. 4-5
III. Prayer for full deliverance v. 6

This psalm is very similar to Psalm 14.

# Psalm 54

**Subject:** A prayer for deliverance from enemies, followed by a profession of confidence in Yahweh
**Author:** David

**Outline**
I. Prayer for deliverance from enemies vv. 1-3
II. Profession of confidence in Yahweh vv. 4-7

# Psalm 55

**Subject:** A prayer for the destruction of wicked and treacherous enemies
**Author:** David

**Outline**
I. Plea to be heard in great distress vv. 1-8
II. Imprecation against treacherous enemies vv. 9-15
III. Statement of trust in God for righteous judgment vv. 16-23

# Psalm 56

**Subject:** A prayer of trust in God for deliverance from danger
**Author:** David

**Outline**
  I.   First prayer of trust in God in the midst of assault vv. 1-4
  II.  Second prayer of trust in God in the midst of assault vv. 5-11
  III. Vow of thanksgiving vv. 12-13

---

# Psalm 57

**Subject:** A prayer of trust in God for deliverance from danger, and praise to God in anticipation of deliverance
**Author:** David

**Outline**
  I.  Prayer for deliverance from enemies vv. 1-5
  II. Praise to God in anticipation of deliverance vv. 6-11

---

# Psalm 58

**Subject:** David remonstrates with the wicked, proving the vileness of their character, praying for their destruction, and finally rejoicing in anticipation of divine vengeance upon them
**Author:** David

**Outline**
  I.   Remonstrance with the wicked vv. 1-2
  II.  Description of the incurably wicked vv. 3-5
  III. Prayer for their destruction vv. 6-9
  IV.  Result of the judgment vv. 10-11
       A. Joy of the righteous v. 10
       B. Testimony to all men v. 11

---

# Psalm 59

**Subject:** A prayer for deliverance from bloodthirsty enemies
**Author:** David

**Outline**
  I.   Cry for deliverance from bloodthirsty men vv. 1-2
  II.  Plea for punishment of unjust assaults vv. 3-5
  III. Description of the attackers vv. 6-7
  IV.  Expression of confidence in God vv. 8-10
  V.   Prayer for exemplary punishment vv. 11-13

VI.   The empty rage of his pursuers vv. 14-15
VII.  Thanksgiving for deliverance vv. 16-17

# Psalm 60

**Subject:** A lament over destruction wrought by an invading force of Edomites, followed by a prayer for victory
**Author:** David

**Outline**
I.    Expostulation with God for abandonment vv. 1-4
II.   Appeal to God's promises vv. 5-8
III.  Prayer of confidence in God vv. 9-12

Apparently Edom made a raid on the land while the army was fighting Aram in the north. David promptly dispatched a force led by Joab, which routed the Edomites. Other Psalms likely written in relation to this event include Psalms 42–43, 61, 79, and 108. Compare 1 Kgs 11:15-16.

Psalms 60–68 comprise perhaps the most beautiful and encouraging portion of the Psalter. There are great descriptions of the blessings of the righteous and their vindication by God. In Psalms 60–67, there is a definite preference for the term "God," rather than "Yahweh," the latter being found only in Psalm 64:10.

# Psalm 61

**Subject:** A prayer for restoration to God's dwelling-place from a faraway and dangerous place, followed by a prayer of thanksgiving in anticipation of the fulfillment of God's promises
**Author:** David

**Outline**
I.    Prayer for restoration to God's dwelling-place vv. 1-4
II.   Prayer of thanks and praise for God's promises vv. 5-8

This psalm is probably a sequel to the preceding one. The king is far from Jerusalem and about to return after answers to prayer—namely, victory over a strong force of Arameans, followed by victory over a strong force of Edomites.

# Psalm 62

**Subject:** A statement of confidence in God as a refuge in the midst of treachery and oppression
**Author:** David

**Outline**
I.    Remonstrance with enemies in light of God's protection vv. 1-4
II.   Statement of confidence in God and exhortation to trust Him vv. 5-8
III.  The vanity of trusting in anything but God vv. 9-12

# Psalm 63

**Subject:** A prayer of satisfaction in God in the midst of a wilderness and enemies
**Author:** David

**Outline**
I. Expression of longing for God's presence vv. 1-2
II. David's continual satisfaction in God vv. 3-6
III. David's protection contrasted with his enemies' destruction vv. 7-9
IV. David's end contrasted with his enemies' vv. 10-11

# Psalm 64

**Subject:** Prayer for deliverance from malicious enemies, and anticipation of their demise
**Author:** David

**Outline**
I. Prayer for deliverance from malicious enemies vv. 1-6
II. Anticipation of his enemies' demise vv. 7-10

# Psalm 65

**Subject:** A hymn of praise to God for His favor to man and to the earth
**Author:** David

**Outline**
I. Invocation of the gathering to praise Yahweh vv. 1-4
II. Israel's God is the confidence of all mankind vv. 5-8
III. Thanksgiving for the harvest vv. 9-13

This psalm was probably composed to be sung at the feast of firstfruits.

# Psalm 66

**Subject:** A psalm of praise and thanksgiving for God's might, His works, and His deliverance of the people and their representative
**Author:** Not stated; from a time when there was a chief musician in Jerusalem

**Outline**
I. Group praise vv. 1-12
    A. Summons to praise God vv. 1-4
    B. Invitation to contemplate God's mighty works vv. 5-7
    C. Praise to God for deliverance of His people vv. 8-12
II. Individual praise vv. 13-20

A. Payment of vows vv. 13-15
B. Invitation to praise God vv. 16-20

# Psalm 67

**Subject:** A prayer for God's blessing on His people, with the result that the nations will join in God's praise
**Author:** Not stated; from a time when there was a chief musician in Jerusalem

## Outline
I. Prayer for God's blessing upon His people vv. 1-2
   A. The request for blessing v. 1
   B. The reason for the blessing v. 2
II. Prayer that the nations might praise God vv. 3-5
   A. The first prayer for the praise of the peoples v. 3
   B. The reason they should praise v. 4
   C. The prayer for praise repeated v. 5
III. Answer to the prayer anticipated vv. 6-7
   A. The blessing anticipated v. 6
   B. The extension of blessing anticipated v. 7

There is an evangelistic aspect to this psalm—God's blessing on Israel is for the purpose that the peoples will be saved and praise Him.

# Psalm 68

**Subject:** A celebration of the march of God to victory, from the establishment of His kingdom in Israel in the past, to the present place of His kingdom in Zion, to the future complete subjugation of all nations
**Author:** David

## Outline
I. Invocation and summons vv. 1-6
II. God's historical choice and defense of His people vv. 7-18
III. God's present help to His people vv. 19-27
IV. God's future subjugation of all nations vv. 28-32
V. Concluding doxology vv. 33-35

This psalm has the highest and most beautiful language in the Psalter. It is the fourth and climactic of a series of four Psalm-songs of David (Pss 65–68). Johnson writes, "The style is abrupt, fragmentary, rugged, astonishingly graphic and forcible, and bespeaks an age of earliest poetry."[47]

---

[47] F. C. Cook, G. H. S. Johnson, and C. J. Elliot, "Psalms." (in *The Holy Bible with an Explanatory and Critical Commentary*, ed. F. C. Cook, vol. 4; Cambridge: C. J. Clay, 1892), 318.

# Psalm 69

**Subject:** A plea for deliverance from enemies, an imprecation against the enemies, and thanksgiving for the anticipated answer
**Author:** David

**Outline**
I. Plea for deliverance from enemies vv. 1-6
II. David's reproach for God's sake vv. 7-12
III. Plea for help vv. 13-18
IV. Imprecation against his adversaries vv. 19-28
V. Praise to God in anticipation of deliverance vv. 29-36

# Psalm 70

**Subject:** A terse prayer for speedy help against persecutors
**Author:** David

**Outline**
I. Plea for help v. 1
II. Imprecation against enemies vv. 2-3
III. Prayer for exaltation of the godly v. 4
IV. Cry for speedy deliverance v. 5

This prayer is a repetition, with minor variations, of Psalm 40:13-17, which is also a psalm of David.

# Psalm 71

**Subject:** Prayer of an old man for deliverance
**Author:** Not stated, but sounds Davidic. In support of this, vv. 1-3 are almost identical to Ps 31:1-3, which is ascribed to David. It would be expected that David might draw upon some of his own compositions when praying for deliverance at the end of his life.

**Outline**
I. Prayer for deliverance vv. 1-13
   A. Prayer of faith in the midst of danger vv. 1-3
   B. Ground for the appeal vv. 4-8
   C. Prayer for deliverance and vindication vv. 9-13
II. Praise for deliverance vv. 14-24
   A. Vows of praise and thanksgiving vv. 14-16
   B. Past faithfulness as ground for present hope vv. 17-20
   C. Thanksgiving for answered prayer vv. 21-24

# Psalm 72

**Subject:** A psalm celebrating the reign of a righteous king who is blessed by God
**Author:** Solomon

**Outline**
   I.  Prayer for divine enablement for the king v. 1
  II.  The righteousness of the king's reign vv. 2-7
 III.  The universal extent of the king's reign vv. 8-11
 IV.  The king's blessedness and blessings vv. 12-17
  V.  Concluding doxology vv. 18-19

---

*Book III – Psalms 73–89 – Psalms by the Temple Singers*

---

# Psalm 73

**Subject:** A didactic psalm that struggles with the problem of evil, contrasting the prosperity of the wicked in this life with their doom in the next and the eternal blessings of the righteous
**Author:** Asaph

**Outline**
   I.  God's goodness to the righteous affirmed v. 1
  II.  The prosperity of the wicked observed vv. 2-12
 III.  Asaph's struggle with the injustices of life vv. 13-17
 IV.  The final doom of the wicked vv. 18-20
  V.  The wisdom of following God vv. 21-28

---

# Psalm 74

**Subject:** A prayer for God to rescue and heal His people after the devastation of the land by an enemy
**Author:** Asaph

**Outline**
   I.  Pleading with God over the desolation of His people vv. 1-11
  II.  God's sovereignty recalled vv. 12-17
 III.  Renewed entreaty to deliver His people vv. 18-23

---

# Psalm 75

**Subject:** God's judgment of the wicked and the proud warned of, and contrasted with the praise and triumph of the righteous
**Author:** Asaph

**Outline**
I.   Corporate thanksgiving to God v. 1
II.  God's assurance of His sovereignty vv. 2-3
III. Warning to wicked boasters vv. 4-8
IV.  The praise and triumph of the righteous vv. 9-10

This is both a Psalm of praise and a didactic Psalm, intended to give the righteous joy and reassurance because of the coming abasement of the proud.

One wonders if this psalm was sung antiphonally, with the choir singing v. 1, a soloist singing vv. 2-3, and another soloist singing vv. 4-10.

# Psalm 76

**Subject:** A celebration of God's absolute triumph in battle, with an admonition to serve and fear Him in response
**Author:** Asaph

**Outline**
I.   The manifestation of God in Zion vv. 1-3
II.  The triumphant return of God from battle vv. 4-6
III. God's irresistible power as Judge and Savior vv. 7-9
IV.  Call to respond in worship vv. 10-12

The arrangement of this psalm in *The Trinity Psalter* is tremendous.

# Psalm 77

**Subject:** In the midst of great distress and unanswered prayer, Asaph recalls the exhibition of God's character and power in the deliverance of His people from Egypt
**Author:** Asaph

**Outline**
I.   Asaph's cry in the midst of trouble vv. 1-3
II.  Asaph's puzzlement over God's inaction vv. 4-9
III. The resolution to recall God's mighty deeds vv. 10-15
IV.  The manifestation of God to deliver His people from Egypt remembered vv. 16-20

The setting for this appears to be national distress, which has caused Asaph personal distress. Most likely it was one of the national difficulties faced during the reign of David.

# Psalm 78

**Subject:** A recitation of Israel's history from the Exodus until David, with a focus on the spiritual lessons to be learned from God's graciousness, Israel's rebellion, and God's judgment
**Author:** Asaph

**Outline**
  I.   Invitation to listen and learn vv. 1-11
  II.  God's works in behalf of Israel in the Exodus and wanderings vv. 12-16
  III. Israel's rebellion in the wilderness vv. 17-20
  IV.  God's judgment vv. 21-31
  V.   Cycles of rebellion, judgment, repentance, and restoration vv. 32-41
  VI.  Remembrance of God's work in the Exodus, the wilderness, and the Conquest vv. 43-55
  VII. Israel's apostasy during the period of judges vv. 56-58
 VIII. God's judgment vv. 59-64
  IX.  God's deliverance of His people through David vv. 65-72

Matthew 13:35 relates this psalm to the revelation of God's kingdom program.

---

# Psalm 79

**Subject:** A prayer for speedy deliverance and restoration after the pillage of Jerusalem
**Author:** Asaph

**Outline**
  I.  The plight of God's people and God's city vv. 1-4
  II. Entreaty for vengeance and restoration vv. 5-13

The authenticity of the attribution to Asaph is assumed to be impossible by nearly all commentators. However, suggestions that deny the historicity do not fit with the contents of the Psalm. The suggestion that the Psalm was composed on the occasion of Jerusalem's destruction by Nebuchadnezzar in 586 B.C. does not fit at all, for this psalm speaks of the defilement of the temple, not its destruction. It is also clear that Israel is still in the land, but under reproach; they have not been carried captive. Cook suggests that both Psalm 74 and Psalm 79 were "composed immediately after the plundering of the temple by Shishak,"[48] a time at which Asaph could theoretically have been yet alive. However, there is no evidence that Shishak actually destroyed most of the buildings in Jerusalem, as this psalm indicates; certainly the temple and palace were not destroyed. The suggestion that this psalm was composed in the Maccabean period is impossible, since the OT canon was closed with the death of the last prophet and the Qumran manuscripts provide direct evidence that the book of Psalms was already in existence before Maccabean times. However, since 1 Samuel 1:9 and 3:3 call the tabernacle "the temple of Yahweh," by analogy, the tent that David pitched for the ark could be called the "temple"; many Davidic psalms do refer to the temple, to the house of God, etc. The occasion of writing was probably the fierce Edomite attack when David and the main army were away from Jerusalem fighting the Arameans.

---

# Psalm 80

**Subject:** A prayer imploring God to rescue and restore His people after suffering great calamities
**Author:** Asaph

---

[48] Cook, "Psalms," 353.

**Outline**
  I.  Summons to God vv. 1-3
 II.  Plea and remonstrance with God vv. 4-7
III.  God's historical care for Israel contrasted with their present brokenness vv. 8-13
 IV.  Prayer for the restoration of God's people vv. 14-19

As with the previous psalm, most commentators assume this was not written by Asaph. However, internal evidence points to the authenticity of the superscription. This psalm represents Israel as one united nation (vv. 8-16), and mentions Joseph, Ephraim, Benjamin, and Manasseh as representative of the entire nation (vv. 1-2). Benjamin was of the southern kingdom, while the other three tribes were of the northern kingdom; the indication is therefore that the nation was not yet divided at this time.

# Psalm 81

**Subject:** A call to celebrate the Feast of Trumpets and Tabernacles, accompanied by a reminder of God's graciousness to Israel and the nation's rebellion against Him
**Author:** Asaph

**Outline**
  I.  Call to celebrate the feast vv. 1-3
 II.  History of the feast vv. 4-7
III.  Terms of the covenant vv. 8-10
 IV.  Israel's refusal to hearken vv. 11-12
  V.  Yahweh's desire to bless His people vv. 13-16

This psalm was intended for public recitation on a festival day (v. 3), probably the Feast of Trumpets.

# Psalm 82

**Subject:** A didactic Psalm which warns against judging unjustly
**Author:** Asaph

**Outline**
  I.  Vision of God as the Judge of judges v. 1
 II.  Admonition to the judges vv. 2-4
III.  Failure of the judges v. 5
 IV.  Judgment of the judges vv. 6-7
  V.  God summoned to judge v. 8

This is an invisible judgment scene, like that of Psalm 50, another Psalm of Asaph.

This psalm stands as a vivid reminder to all who are in authority that they have a higher authority to whom they must answer. They are gods, yes, but there is a Most High God above them who will hold them accountable. They ought to rule and judge righteously, for they are mortal and will face judgment after they perish.

# Psalm 83

**Subject:** Prayer for the judgment of the nations which have gathered together to cut off Israel
**Author:** Asaph

## Outline
   I.  Prayer for God to act while many nations assault Israel vv. 1-8
      A. Prayer for God to rescue His people vv. 1-4
      B. Enumeration of the confederate peoples v. 5-8
  II.  Prayer for God to destroy the nations and exalt Himself vv. 9-18
      A. Prayer for God to act in the present as He has in the past vv. 9-12
      B. Specific prayer for retribution and vindication vv. 13-18

# Psalm 84

**Subject:** A prayer in which the Psalmist expresses the greatness of his affection for the house of Yahweh
**Author:** One of the sons of Korah

## Outline
    I.  The Psalmist's longing for the house of Yahweh vv. 1-3
   II.  The blessedness of those who dwell in the house of Yahweh vv. 4-7
  III.  The Psalmist's request vv. 8-10
  IV.  The privilege of closeness to God vv. 11-12

# Psalm 85

**Subject:** A prayer for God's revival of the nation after their restoration from previous troubles. God's blessing is assured, but on the condition that the people do not commit the same sins that brought God's judgment upon their fathers.
**Author:** One of the sons of Korah

## Outline
    I.  God's restoration of Israel declared vv. 1-3
   II.  Prayer for revival vv. 4-7
  III.  Assurance of God's blessing upon the penitent nation vv. 8-13

This psalm is pre-exilic. There were sons of Korah who returned from the exile, but this is in the earlier collection of psalms; the expression שַׁבְתָּ שְׁבוּת יַעֲקֹב (v. 1[E] / v. 2[MT]) does not necessarily speak of the Babylonian exile and return, but is rather a stock expression that refers to the restoration of fortunes after calamity (cf. Job 42:10).

# Psalm 86

**Subject:** Prayer for mercy and deliverance from wicked adversaries, accompanied by prayers of adoration and commitment
**Author:** David

## Outline
  I. Prayer for restoration vv. 1-7
 II. Prayer of adoration vv. 8-10
III. Prayer of commitment vv. 11-13
 IV. Prayer for deliverance vv. 14-17

This is the only Psalm attributed to David in Book III.

---

# Psalm 87

**Subject:** The glories of Zion extolled
**Author:** One of the sons of Korah

## Outline
  I. Zion glorified as the city of God vv. 1-3
 II. Zion glorified as the head of the nations vv. 4-6
III. Zion glorified as the source of joy and life v. 7

---

# Psalm 88

**Subject:** Distressed prayer to be delivered from death
**Author:** Heman the Ezrahite, one of the temple singers

## Outline
  I. The desperation of Heman's plight vv. 1-8
     A. Petition to be heard vv. 1-2
     B. Personal troubles vv. 3-7
     C. Isolation from friends v. 8
 II. Heman's plea to be saved from death vv. 9-13
III. Heman's complaint vv. 14-18

First Chronicles 15:19 identifies Heman, Asaph, and Ethan as the three chief singers when David brought the ark to Jerusalem.

Kirkpatrick calls this "the saddest Psalm in the whole Psalter."[49] Heman is staring death in the face after a period of unrelieved suffering. There is no note of praise at the end of the Psalm in anticipation of deliverance. In fact, there is nothing positive at all said in this psalm; Heman's only mood is despair and desperation. It is notable that Heman never doubts God or His goodness in the midst of his dire straits.

---

[49] Kirkpatrick, *Psalms*, 523.

# Psalm 89

**Subject:** Plea to deliver Israel on the basis of God's incomparable greatness and the covenant He made with David

**Author:** Ethan the Ezrahite, one of the temple singers

**Outline**
 I. The Psalmist's theme stated vv. 1-4
 II. The greatness of Yahweh celebrated vv. 5-18
   A. His power and faithfulness vv. 5-13
   B. His goodness to His people vv. 14-18
 III. The Davidic Covenant recounted vv. 19-37
   A. The promise to David personally vv. 19-28
   B. The promise to David's seed vv. 29-37
 IV. Plea to deliver Israel vv. 38-51
 V. Concluding doxology v. 52

This psalm may have been composed near the end of Ethan's life, early in the reign of Rehoboam, after the invasion of Shishak. The only other possibility would be Absalom's rebellion.

---

*Book IV – Psalms 90–106 – Psalms of God's Care for Israel*

---

# Psalm 90

**Subject:** A prayer for the restoration of God's favor to His people, following a contrast of God's eternality and sovereignty with man's frailty and mortality

**Author:** Moses

**Outline**
 I. Confession of God as the supreme, eternal Lord vv. 1-6
 II. Lament over the transitory nature of the Israelites' lives vv. 7-12
 III. Prayer for a restoration of divine favor vv. 13-17

This psalm was composed as a reflection on the forty years of wilderness wanderings, in which the people fell down slain under the wrath of God like grasshoppers. Every person over the age of twenty met a divinely ordained death within thirty-eight years after Sinai.

This is likely the oldest Psalm in the Psalter.

Every verse in this psalm ends with a period. These are simple, profound thoughts.

---

# Psalm 91

**Subject:** The security, at all times, of the man who puts His trust in God.[50]

---

**Author:** Not stated; see Elliot, "Psalms," 506-12, who argues that Isaiah may have written Psalms 91–100, or at least Psalms 93–100. The problem with this is, the NT attributes the authorship of Psalm 95 to David.

**Outline**
   I. The Psalmist's boast of confidence in God vv. 1-4
  II. The assurance of safety from all perils to him who trusts in God vv. 5-13
 III. The divine response: confirmation of the promise vv. 14-16

This psalm is difficult to understand because it is obvious that evil things befall every righteous person who has ever lived. Indeed, this sounds very much like the prosperity theology expressed by Eliphaz in the book of Job (cf. Job 5:17-27). However, the statements in this psalm are in fact true if properly qualified, as affirmed even by Elihu in Job 36. Psalm 91 states the general expectation of how God will treat the righteous, without all the caveats that we might add. Yes, there are many exceptions to the general rule, but this is generally how things go for the righteous on the earth.

# Psalm 92

**Subject:** "The faithfulness and truth of God as displayed in His righteous administration of the universe, and as vindicated by the ultimate destiny both of the righteous and the wicked."[51]
**Author:** not stated

**Outline**
   I. The joy of continually praising Yahweh vv. 1-3
  II. The sovereignty of Yahweh as grounds for praise vv. 4-8
 III. The demise of Yahweh's enemies and the blessings Yahweh's servants vv. 9-15

There are some textual problems associated Pss 92–99, probably due to the lack of superscriptions. "Ps. xciii. is a part of Ps. xcii. in twelve Codices, Ps. xcv. is joined to Ps. xciv. in nine Codices, Ps. xcvi. is a part of Ps. xcv. in four Codices, Ps. xcvii. is a part of Ps. xcvi. in fourteen Codices, and Ps. xcix. is united with Ps. xcvii. in eight Codices."[52] The divisions of these psalms in English Bibles is best regarded as correct.

# Psalm 93

**Subject:** A celebration of Yahweh's kingdom reign
**Author:** not stated

**Outline**
   I. Celebration of Yahweh's reign over the earth vv. 1-2
  II. Celebration of Yahweh's supremacy over the nations vv. 3-4

---

[50] Adapted from Elliot, "Psalms," 376.

[51] C. J. Elliot, "Psalms," 379.

[52] C. J. Elliot, "Psalms," 506. This quote has been modified to omit repeated uses of the word "that."

III. Celebration of the holiness of Yahweh's reign v. 5

That this psalm is speaking of the millennial kingdom is demonstrated by a comparison of v. 1 with 96:10. It is a celebration of Yahweh's "personal manifestation of Himself as the King of the whole earth."[53]

---

# Psalm 94

**Subject:** A prayer for Yahweh to judge the earth
**Author:** not stated

## Outline
I. Yahweh's judgment of the wicked vv. 1-11
    A. Yahweh summoned to judge the earth vv. 1-2
    B. Complaint over Yahweh's delay vv. 3-7
    C. The folly of denying the fact of judgment vv. 8-11
II. Yahweh's comfort to the righteous vv. 12-23
    A. Yahweh's merciful dealings with His people vv. 12-15
    B. Yahweh the Psalmist's comfort and confidence vv. 16-19
    C. Confidence in the ultimate triumph of justice vv. 20-23

This psalm is the OT version of "Thy kingdom come," a prayer for the second advent.

---

# Psalm 95

**Subject:** Description of Yahweh's praise and reign in the messianic kingdom, followed by a call to enter the kingdom
**Author:** Not stated; Hebrews 4:7 attributes to David, probably based on the LXX superscription. However, the argument of Hebrews would still be valid if Psalm 95 were composed later than the time of David, perhaps by Isaiah in the seventh century. Actually, a later date would only serve to reinforce the argument of Hebrews 4, since the point made in that chapter is that there was a long gap of time between the original message to the wilderness generation and the composition of Psalm 95.

## Outline
I. Call to worship Yahweh in the kingdom vv. 1-7b
II. Call to enter the kingdom vv. 7c-11

Verses 1-7b are written from the perspective of someone who is living in the kingdom, while verses 7c-11 are an exhortation to be saved so as to enter the kingdom.

Historically, Jewish commentators interpreted Psalms 95–100 as messianic.[54] There can be no doubt that this interpretation is correct. The Psalmist prophetically sees the messianic kingdom and describes it. See comments on these individual psalms for elaboration. It is no wonder, though, that the messianic

---

[53] Elliot, "Psalms," 382.

[54] C. J. Elliot, "Psalms," 387.

interpretation of these psalms has never been popular in the church. Throughout the Middle Ages and the Reformation, nearly the entire church rejected the concept of a literal millennium. In modern times, evangelical authors have been strongly influenced by the liberal claim that there is no such thing as a direct prophecy, and as a result attempt to find in these psalms a setting in the author's own time. Thus, these psalms have basically never been properly understood by the church.

# Psalm 96

**Subject:** A call to worship Yahweh the Righteous Judge in the messianic kingdom
**Author:** not stated

**Outline**
   I.  Call for universal worship of Yahweh vv. 1-3
  II.  Reasons to worship Yahweh vv. 4-6
 III.  Call to proclaim Yahweh's greatness vv. 7-10
 IV.  Call for nature to rejoice vv. 11-12
  V.  The coming of the kingdom anticipated v. 13

This is the second in the series of psalms regarding the messianic kingdom. Note the repeated references to all peoples in the earth praising Yahweh and serving Yahweh. Verses 10-13 are especially clear descriptions of the Messiah's kingdom reign.

This psalm contains parallels to 1 Chronicles 16 and Psalm 98.

# Psalm 97

**Subject:** A description of Yahweh's reign in the messianic kingdom, with an emphasis on Yahweh's triumph and a call for a response
**Author:** not stated

**Outline**
   I.  The reign of Yahweh proclaimed vv. 1-3
  II.  The coming of Yahweh recounted vv. 4-5
 III.  The triumph of Yahweh proclaimed vv. 7-9
 IV.  Call for a response to the promise vv. 10-12

This is another prophetic Psalm. Verses 1-9 are written from the viewpoint of a person in the messianic kingdom. The reign of Yahweh and His destruction of the wicked at the second coming are recounted. The second coming is described in the past tense, while Yahweh's reign is in the present tense. Verses 10-12 return to the perspective of this present age, encouraging the righteous to live with the kingdom in view.

Incidentally, the references to Yahweh reigning in the messianic kingdom show that the Messiah is Yahweh.

# Psalm 98

**Subject:** A call to praise Yahweh in the messianic kingdom

**Author:** not stated

**Outline**

I. Call for a new song v. 1a
II. Reason for the song vv. 1b-3
III. Call for man to sing to Yahweh vv. 4-6
IV. Call for nature to sing to Yahweh vv. 7-8
V. Reason for the song v. 9

This is another prophetic Psalm, written from a kingdom perspective. Verses 1-8 are written as if the Psalmist is in the kingdom, while v. 9 returns to the perspective of this present age and looks ahead to the future. The language of v. 8 is quite similar to Isaiah 55:12, which describes conditions in the kingdom.

# Psalm 99

**Subject:** A proclamation of the reign of Yahweh in the messianic kingdom, and a call for praise in response
**Author:** not stated

**Outline**

I. First proclamation of Yahweh's reign vv. 1-2
II. First call for praise v. 3
III. Second proclamation of Yahweh's reign v. 4
IV. Second call for praise v. 5
V. The vindication of Yahweh's servants vv. 6-8
VI. Third call for praise v. 9

This is another Psalm of the messianic kingdom, written from the perspective of someone who is in the kingdom. The emphasis in this psalm is on the fulfillment of Yahweh's promises to Israel.

# Psalm 100

**Subject:** A psalm of thanksgiving to Yahweh from the perspective of the messianic kingdom
**Author:** not stated

**Outline**

I. Universal call to praise Yahweh vv. 1-2
II. Call to acknowledge Yahweh's greatness v. 3
III. Call to worship renewed v. 4
IV. Reasons for the praise v. 5

This psalm is universal in its scope, and does not contain any specific references to Israel. It is therefore likely that it continues the same subject of the previous five psalms, that of the millennial kingdom. It describes the thankful worship of Yahweh in the kingdom by all the nations of the earth. Once again, it appears to be written from the perspective of someone who is living in the kingdom.

This is one of the best known of the psalms, and it always has been so. It has always had a prominent place in the liturgy of the Christian church, and few tunes are more familiar than Old Hundredth.

# Psalm 101

**Subject:** The king's pledge to rule Israel in righteousness
**Author:** David

**Outline**

I. David's pledge to holiness in relation to himself and God vv. 1-4
II. David's pledge to holiness in relation to his fellow man vv. 5-8

# Psalm 102

**Subject:** A prayer for God's mercy on the afflicted individual and his people, followed by the anticipation of Zion's restoration through the faithfulness of the eternal God
**Author:** not stated

**Outline**

I. The Psalmist's complaint vv. 1-11
II. The Psalmist's anticipation of Zion's restoration vv. 12-22
III. The Psalmist's comfort in God's immutability vv. 23-28

It is evident that this psalm was written in reaction to some tragedy that befell Zion, perhaps accompanied by some further personal affliction suffered by the Psalmist. One suggestion is that Jerusalem had been destroyed and the Psalmist was in captivity. This is supported by the reference to the "stones" and "dust" of Jerusalem in v. 14, along with the reference to the "set time" (מוֹעֵד) of the city's restoration in v. 13, i.e., the end of the seventy years. Currently the Psalmist and his companions are destitute (v. 17) and look forward to the day when men will again sing Yahweh's praises in Jerusalem (v. 21). On the other hand, the placement of this psalm in Book IV suggest a pre-exilic setting.

Verses 19-22 look forward to the ultimate day of Zion's restoration in the millennial kingdom. The Psalmist then acknowledges that while he is weak and his days are shortened, the eternal God will not fail His people, but will bring about Zion's final restoration at the appointed time when He returns to set up His kingdom (vv. 23-28). Hebrews 1:10-12 properly interprets vv. 25-27 as a reference to the Son because of the allusion to the second advent and the restoration of the Davidic monarchy in Zion in v. 28.

# Psalm 103

**Subject:** A call to bless Yahweh for His graciousness
**Author:** David

**Outline**

I. David summons his soul to bless Yahweh vv. 1-5
II. Yahweh's graciousness illustrated from the history of His people vv. 6-10
III. The greatness of Yahweh's graciousness vv. 11-14
IV. Human temporality contrasted with Yahweh's graciousness vv. 15-18
V. A call for all creation to bless Yahweh vv. 19-22

# Psalm 104

**Subject:** A hymn of praise to God for His sovereignty over nature
**Author:** not stated

**Outline**
 I. Summons to praise v. 1a
 II. God's greatness as Creator extolled vv. 1b-5
 III. God's greatness in sending the flood extolled vv. 6-9
 IV. God's wisdom in making the earth habitable extolled vv. 10-24
   A. God's provision of food in the earth vv. 10-18
   B. God's establishment of temporal cycles for the earth vv. 19-23
   C. Doxology v. 24
 V. The dependence of all upon God observed vv. 25-30
 VI. Closing doxology vv. 31-35

This psalm is notable for not having any specific historical or geographical referents, except to the cedars of Lebanon (v. 16). There is no mention of Israel, David, Zion, the temple, or a king. The language sounds Davidic, though, and the psalm begins and ends with the same formula as the previous (Davidic) psalm.

# Psalm 105

**Subject:** Yahweh praised for His wondrous works in behalf of Israel
**Author:** not stated

**Outline**
 I. Call to praise Yahweh and declare His works vv. 1-7
 II. Yahweh's covenant with the patriarchs vv. 8-15
 III. Yahweh's faithfulness to Israel in Egypt vv. 16-24
 IV. Yahweh's deliverance of Israel from Egypt vv. 25-38
 V. Yahweh's care for Israel in the wilderness vv. 39-43
 VI. Yahweh's establishment of Israel in the land vv. 44-45

Verses 1-15 are paralleled in 1 Chronicles 16:8-22, which was sung by Asaph and his brethren at David's command.

# Psalm 106

**Subject:** A confession of Israel's history of rebellion against God, and a prayer for the restoration of divine favor
**Author:** not stated

**Outline**
 I. Opening doxology vv. 1-3
 II. Prayer for restoration of blessing vv. 4-5

III. Israel's history of rebellion and chastisement vv. 6-46
    A. Confession of sin by the present generation v. 6
    B. Israel's rebellion in the wilderness vv. 7-33
    C. Israel's rebellion in the land vv. 34-46
IV. Prayer for deliverance from the nations v. 47
 V. Concluding doxology v. 48

This psalm is a sequel to the preceding one, reciting Israel's history from the Exodus through the period of the judges, with a focus on Israel's rebelliousness in spite of God's repeated wondrous works—in contrast to Ps 105, which focuses solely on the wondrous works. There is no mention of David, but the psalm appears to have been written in David's time, shortly after the period of the judges had ended.

Parts of this psalm (vv. 1, 47-48) are paralleled in 1 Chronicles 16, which was sung by Asaph and his brethren at the command of David. Importantly, this includes the prayer to be gathered together and delivered from the nations (with slightly different wording), which shows that v. 47 is not necessarily reflective of an exilic situation. Verse 6 could be read as a confession of sin by the exilic community, although it could just as easily have been prayed during the period of the monarchy.

---

*Book V – Psalms 107–150 – Psalms for Special Liturgical Use*

---

# Psalm 107

**Subject:** A call to thank Yahweh because of His deliverance of men from distress and His providential governance of the world

**Author:** not stated

### Outline
  I. Exhortation to thank Yahweh for His deliverance from troubles vv. 1-3
 II. Examples of deliverance from troubles vv. 4-32
    A. The deliverance of travelers from desert perils vv. 4-9
    B. The deliverance of chastised sinners from bonds vv. 10-16
    C. The deliverance of chastised fools from illness vv. 17-22
    D. The deliverance of seafarers from great storms vv. 23-32
III. God's providence in the vicissitudes of men's fortunes vv. 33-43

Some commentators understand each of the examples in vv. 4-32 to be references to events in Israel's history, but it seems better to view them as general statements of providence.

---

# Psalm 108

**Subject:** David praises God, then appeals to His promises for deliverance from enemies and expresses confidence in God's help

**Author:** David

### Outline
  I. Praise to God in anticipation of deliverance vv. 1-5

II. Appeal to God's promises vv. 6-10
III. Prayer of faith for deliverance vv. 11-13

This psalm consists of the last five verses of Psalm 57 and the last eight of Psalm 60, which are also ascribed to David. The occasion of writing is the same as that for Psalm 60.

# Psalm 109

**Subject:** A prayer for God's punishment of David's adversaries in retribution for their unjust and malicious treatment of him
**Author:** David

**Outline**
  I. David's innocence protested vv. 1-5
 II. Prayer for retribution upon David's chief persecutor vv. 6-20
III. Prayer for God's mercy upon David vv. 21-31

David has been betrayed by one of his close associates, and he prays for God's deliverance of himself and punishment of his adversary.

# Psalm 110

**Subject:** A prophetic psalm of praise which extols Jesus Christ as the divine King-Priest
**Author:** David

**Outline**
  I. The Messiah's future reign vv. 1-3
 II. The Messiah's exaltation to an everlasting priesthood v. 4
III. The Messiah's seizure of power vv. 5-7

vv. 1-3 are about the Messiah's promised dominion
v. 4 is the center of the psalm
vv. 5-7 are about the Messiah's destruction of His enemies

Psalm 110 is set near the beginning of Book V of the Psalter (Psalms 107–150), which was likely compiled by Ezra for liturgical use on special occasions. Psalm 110 is the final and climactic of the four Davidic psalms of deliverance which open Book V (Psalms 107–110). After three lengthy, impassioned cries for God's deliverance in Psalms 107, 108, and 109, the Psalmist jumps ahead to the final resolution of all the conflicts of all the saints in Psalm 110, which describes the exaltation of the messianic King-Priest and His seizure of power over the world. The acrostic Psalm 111 begins a new section of Book V, but it sounds like an outburst of praise to Yahweh after the grand vision of the Messiah's exaltation and rule in Psalm 110.
Psalm 110 is a prophetic vision of the Messiah's seizure of power over the world, which is described by David in the Spirit (cf. 2 Sam 23:2; Matt 22:43). As the prototypical king of Israel and the human progenitor of Christ, David also prophesied of Christ in a number of other psalms (e.g., Pss 2, 16, 22). Psalm 110 opens with a vision of the Messiah's triumphant seating in heaven at the right hand of God, awaiting future conquest (v. 1)—an event which we know from the New Testament occurred when Jesus

ascended to heaven forty days after His resurrection (cf. Acts 2:34-35). Christ is then addressed in v. 2, and is given an invitation and a promise that Yahweh (the Father) will establish His rule over His enemies. The preparation for the Messiah's conquest is described in v. 3: when the Lord comes to earth in great strength and vitality to seize power, He will be accompanied by an army of followers who are clad in holy garments. The reason why Christ's followers are holy is that He is an eternal priest after the order of Melchizedek, as God the Father declares Him to be with an oath in v. 4. Verses 5-7 describe prophetically, in the third person, the actions of the Messiah as He subdues His enemies and establishes His eternal kingdom. The event at which Christ destroys His enemies is what we know as the second coming/second advent, which occurs at the end of the seven-year tribulation period (Rev 19:11-21). The universal rule which Christ establishes afterward is what we call the millennium, after the thousand years of Revelation 20, though in fact Christ's kingdom is not destroyed at the end of the thousand years, but continues on for all eternity.

Although every one of the psalms is important, Psalm 110 may be the most critical of all, for it is the most-quoted psalm in the New Testament. The NT citations are as follows:
- Matt 22:41-46 quotes v. 1 and applies it specifically to a Messiah who is divine.
- Mark 12:35-37 quotes v. 1 in the same context.
- Luke 20:41-44 quotes v. 1 in the same context.
- Acts 2:34-35 quotes v. 1 as a messianic prophecy that was fulfilled at the ascension.
- 1 Cor 15:25 alludes to v. 1.
- Heb 1:13 quotes v. 1 in the context of messianic prophecies
- Heb 5:6 and 7:17, 21 are direct quotes of v. 4.
- Hebrews contains numerous references to Jesus becoming a high priest after the order of Melchizedek, each of which is an allusion to v. 4.
- Heb 10:12-13 alludes to v. 1
- Christ is said to be seated at God's right hand in Matt 26:64; Mark 14:62; Luke 22:69; Eph 1:20-22; Heb 1:3; 12:2; 1 Pet 3:22.

Psalm 110 was the favorite psalm of Martin Luther, who considered it "of all the psalms the very crown and chief."[55]

Psalm 110 is one of the key messianic prophecies in the OT. Of all the passages in the OT that witness to the divinity of the Messiah, Jesus appealed to Psalm 110 as the clearest possible statement. In the middle of the Passion Week, Jesus used Psalm 110:1 to pin the Pharisees on the all-important question of the identity of the Messiah. Whose Son was the Messiah? The Pharisees claimed that the Messiah was the son of David, i.e., a genetic descendant of David, and had rejected Jesus on the basis that He claimed to be the divine Son of God (Matt 26:63-66; Mark 14:61-64; Luke 22:70-71; John 5:17-18; 10:24-39; 19:7).[56] This is why Psalm 110:1 is so powerful: it shows that the Messiah has to be divine, since the only "Son" who could be the Lord of Israel's greatest king—and therefore already in existence at the time David wrote Psalm 110—is the divine Son of God. The Pharisees had no exegetical basis for denying this conclusion, but to admit it would be to admit that their stated reason for rejecting Jesus' claim to

---

[55] F. C. Cook, G. H. S. Johnson, and C. J. Elliot, "Psalms." (in *The Holy Bible with an Explanatory and Critical Commentary*, ed. F. C. Cook, vol. 4; Cambridge: C. J. Clay, 1892), 429.

[56] In the book of Revelation (22:16), Jesus identifies himself as "the root and the offspring of David." If the house of David is represented as a tree, Christ is both the root of the tree and a branch from it. In this discussion with the Pharisees, Jesus does not deny that the Messiah is David's Son in some sense, but He does emphatically deny that the Messiah is a genetic descendant of David. Jesus' legal father was in the Davidic line, but Jesus was conceived by the Holy Spirit in Mary's womb, apart from any genetic contribution from either Mary or Joseph.

messiahship was simply wrong. With brilliant minds but harder hearts, they literally had nothing to say in reply.

Psalm 110 is also critical because it gives a clear statement and definition of the Messiah's priestly function—He is an eternal Priest after the order of Melchizedek. The author of Hebrews draws out the profound implications in Heb 7: a return to the Melchizedekian priesthood implies an intention to do away with the Levitical priesthood, and in particular with the high priest.[57] The Mosaic Law made no provision for a Melchizedekian high priesthood, so if a new priesthood is introduced, the Law must be changed or terminated. Psalm 110 and Zech 6:13 are the two passages which most clearly describe the Messiah as a King-Priest. The kingly aspect was focused upon by the Jews, who did not see the need for the Messiah to make atonement for the people with His own blood, or to found a priesthood of a different order.

The interpretive key to Psalm 110 is its superscription, which attributes authorship of the Psalm to David. Most modern scholars deny that Psalm 110 is speaking of the divine Messiah, but they must deny Davidic authorship to do so, which means denying the inerrancy of the biblical text—not just the authority of the superscription in the Hebrew text, but also the attribution of Psalm 110 to David by Jesus in the Gospels, and by Peter in Acts. Jesus' entire argument would be invalid if David did not write Psalm 110. The reason why the Pharisees were silenced by Jesus' argument is that they accepted the inerrancy of the biblical text, and therefore accepted Davidic authorship of Psalm 110. If David wrote Psalm 110, it *has* to be speaking of the divine Messiah, for there is no one else whom David would call "my Lord."

If Davidic authorship is accepted, then the date of composition of this psalm must be sometime during the reign of David, sometime after the Davidic Covenant was given. From this perspective, there is no "life-setting" (*Sitz im Leben*) of the psalm, *per se*, since that would imply that it refers to historical events concurrent with the time of writing. Liberal theologians propose no less than ten different life-settings, for they do not know what to make of a psalm that is simply a straight prophecy.

Liberals start, as always, with the assumption that the Bible is a human product and does not contain prophecies. They deny Davidic authorship of this psalm because they cannot imagine King David calling another man "my Lord"—therefore, they conclude, the psalm must have been written about David or some other king by a court poet. Of course, there is no basis for their view other than their own theological precommitment, since they have to deny what is actually written.

Progressive dispensationalists, under the influence of liberal-critical scholarship, start with the assumptions that every prophecy has a near-term historical referent, and that the Jews were unitarian in pre-Christian times. They also deny Davidic authorship, and interpret Psalm 110 form-critically as a "royal psalm," describing the coronation of some human king in metaphorical terms that are literally realized by the Messiah. But there is a powerful argument against the PD interpretation of Psalm 110: Hebrews 7 states plainly that the Melchizedekian priesthood cannot function simultaneously with the Levitical priesthood. Bock argues that "the reference to the priesthood looks back to the Jebusite ancestry of the Jerusalem kingship (cf. Gen 14)."[58] However, Psalm 110:4 is not a historical reference to Melchizedek, but refers instead to the anointing of a new priest after the order of Melchizedek. In addition, his priesthood is forever, which could not apply in any way to a mortal man. David never occupied the Melchizedekian priesthood, and the Davidic king Uzziah was smitten with leprosy for taking the priestly role upon himself.

---

[57] Ezekiel 40–48 describes a functioning priesthood in the millennium, but it is a Zadokite priesthood, rather than an Aaronic priesthood, and there is no mention of a high priest anywhere in these chapters, since Jesus is now the High Priest after the Melchizedekian order. Thus, the priestly system that is in effect in the millennium is not the one ordained by Moses in the Law.

[58] Darrell L. Bock, *Proclamation from Prophecy and Pattern: Lucan Old Testament Christology* (*JSNT* 12; Worcester: Sheffield Academic, 1987), 129.

The arguments of both liberals and progressive dispensationalists against the messianic reading of Psalm 110 are somewhat disingenuous, because they are not basing their view on the content or context of Psalm 110 itself, but on their theological presuppositions—and they are trying to find a way to read Psalm 110 within the context of their presuppositions. It is quite impossible to take this text literally, and to interpret it historically, with the King as someone other than a divine Person. Jesus specifically says that it is impossible for it to refer to a merely human son of David. Other interpretations are incredulous—Allen, for example, suggests in the revised WBC that v. 1 refers to Bathsheba sitting at David's right hand. This would mean that David is identified as Yahweh—a totally preposterous and blasphemous idea. The Midrash to Psalm 110 interprets the king as Abraham. The problem is, the messianic promises were to David's son, and it was a descendant of David who was to have rule over Israel and the world in the messianic kingdom. An alternative interpretation in the Midrash states that David was sitting at God's right hand waiting for Saul to die so he could assume the throne. The obvious problem with this, aside from the fact that David did not literally sit at God's right hand during his lifetime, is that David calls the person at God's right hand "my lord." David was not his own lord. There is no place in the OT where a king calls himself "my lord." There also was no human king who occupied the Melchizedekian priesthood forever. The bottom line is, the inerrancy and authority of the biblical text must be denied in order to deny that Psalm 110 refers to the divine Messiah. The Pharisees were the leading scholars of their day, and they specialized in allegorical interpretation, yet they could not think of any way to get out of Jesus' question by introducing a historical or metaphorical fulfillment. Modern scholars can only take this interpretation from a non-inerrantist perspective, denying the authority of the Bible and the possibility of the supernatural. They are not more clever than the Pharisees, but are actually more dense, because they have denied the authority of Scripture.

# Psalm 111

**Subject:** Yahweh is praised for His works
**Author:** not stated

## Outline

This is an acrostic Psalm, in which each colon (subdivision of a verse) but the first begins with a successive letter of the Hebrew alphabet. As such, it is the acrostic that gives structure to the psalm, which otherwise follows a theme rather than an outline. Even though Psalm 111 is only ten verses, it contains twenty-two cola, in addition to a heading.

# Psalm 112

**Subject:** The welfare of the man who fears Yahweh
**Author:** not stated

## Outline

As with Psalm 111, this is an acrostic Psalm, in which each colon (subdivision of a verse) but the first begins with a successive letter of the Hebrew alphabet. As such, it is the acrostic that gives structure to the psalm, which otherwise follows a theme rather than an outline. Even though Psalm 111 is only ten verses, it contains twenty-two cola, in addition to a heading.

# Psalm 113

**Subject:** "A call to praise Jehovah, Who, though enthroned in majesty in heaven, condescends to care for the weak and lowly on the earth."[59]
**Author:** not stated

## Outline
I. Call to praise Yahweh vv. 1-3
II. Yahweh praised for His glory and condescension vv. 4-6
III. Yahweh praised for His exaltation of the lowly vv. 7-9

# Psalm 114

**Subject:** Celebration of God's power in delivering His people from Egypt
**Author:** not stated

## Outline
I. The Exodus as Israel's defining national event vv. 1-2
II. Demonstration of power over nature in the route from Egypt to Canaan vv. 3-4
III. Nature queried as to its behavior vv. 5-6
IV. Call to fear the God of Jacob vv. 7-8

God is dramatically not mentioned in this psalm until v. 7.

# Psalm 115

**Subject:** A vindication of Yahweh as the one true God
**Author:** not stated

## Outline
I. Call for Yahweh to act in behalf of His people vv. 1-3
II. The folly of trusting in idols vv. 4-8
III. Call to trust in Yahweh vv. 9-11
IV. The blessings of Yahweh upon His people vv. 12-15
V. Resolution to praise Yahweh vv. 16-18

The mockery of idols in this psalm sounds much like Isaiah, and many verses in this psalm are very similar to Isaiah. The psalm may have been written by Isaiah. This is supported by the reference to "the house of Aaron" in v. 12, likely identifying the author as a priest. Note that vv. 4-8 are identical to Psalm 135:15-18.

---

[59] Kirkpatrick, *Psalms*, 677.

# Psalm 116

**Subject:** A psalm of thanksgiving and consecration in response to deliverance from imminent danger of death
**Author:** not stated

**Outline**
  I. The Psalmist's present devotion in response to past deliverance vv. 1-4
 II. God's gracious dealings with the Psalmist vv. 5-9
III. The Psalmist's resolution to serve God vv. 10-19

This psalm is good to preach for a Thanksgiving sermon.

---

# Psalm 117

**Subject:** This is a brief exhortation for the Gentiles to praise Yahweh because of who He is and what He has done for them.
**Author:** not stated

**Outline**
  I. Exhortation for the nations to praise Yahweh v. 1
 II. Reasons to praise Yahweh v. 2a-b
III. Concluding exhortation v. 2c

This, the shortest of all the Psalms, is a universal call to praise God, not just in good times, but for who He is and for what He has already done. It is noteworthy as an OT exhortation to the Gentiles—something that catches the apostle Paul's attention in Romans 15:11.

---

# Psalm 118

**Subject:** An antiphonal song of thanksgiving to be sung in a procession to the temple on some festal occasion during the life of David
**Author:** Not stated, but the first person references could only have been spoken by David

**Outline**
   I. Call to thank Yahweh for His lovingkindness vv. 1-4
  II. Yahweh acclaimed as David's Confidence vv. 5-9
 III. Yahweh praised for helping David in war vv. 10-14
  IV. Yahweh praised for saving and gladdening His people vv. 15-16
   V. Yahweh praised for preserving the life of David vv. 17-18
  VI. Call to enter into the temple gates vv. 19-21
 VII. Yahweh acclaimed for His choice of David vv. 22-24
VIII. Yahweh entreated to bless the people through David v. 25
  IX. David blessed by the temple singers v. 26
   X. The sacrifice presented to Yahweh v. 27
  XI. Concluding doxology vv. 28-29

This psalm utilizes an interesting literary form that could be called "dual parallelism." That is, two or more parallel sets of cola are parallel to each other. These sets of parallel cola are found in vv. 1-4, 5-7, 8-9, 10-12, 13-14, 15-16, 17-18, 19-21, 22-24?, 25-27?, 28-29. Each set of cola is united by a prominent thought.

This psalm sounds thoroughly Davidic, and the messianic references in vv. 22-26 would almost mandate that it be Davidic. Verse 10, for example, sounds like a saying of David, and certainly does not sound postexilic. That the entire Psalm is not directly messianic is proved by the reference to chastening in v. 18. The "I" parts of this psalm were sung by King David as he led the procession to the temple. There definitely were porters at the time of David, even though the temple had not yet been built. Murphy suggests that this psalm was composed for a feast day, perhaps the Passover following the establishment of the Davidic Covenant.

"The Psalm was evidently intended to be sung by the procession of worshippers on their way to the Temple upon some special occasion of national rejoicing. Doubtless it was sung antiphonally, in the manner described in Ezra iii. 11, choir answering choir: but the precise distribution of the parts between the different choirs or voices cannot be determined with certainty."[60] Kirkpatrick suggests that the procession approaches the temple gates in vv. 19-20, with the procession singing v. 19 and the porters or Levites within the temple singing v. 20. David responds with v. 21 as he enters, giving the reason why He is thankful to Yahweh. Verse 26 was originally an acclamation of David as he entered the temple courts, sung antiphonally by a choir of Levites. The sacrifice is prepared in v. 27.

The outline of the Psalm should follow the parts of the speakers, as indicated by the grammar. Likely the procession went from the king's palace to the temple mount.

---

# Psalm 119

**Subject:** A personal meditation and prayer regarding the law of God
**Author:** not stated

## Outline

This psalm is a repeating stanzaic acrostic, arranged in twenty-two stanzas, each of which has eight lines that begin with a single letter of the Hebrew alphabet. These twenty-two stanzas are usually marked in English Bibles by the letters that the lines in each stanza begin with. It is the acrostic that gives structure to the psalm, which otherwise follows a theme rather than an outline. Kugel notes that "In some biblical alphabets such as Psalm 119 one may observe a marked weakening of semantic parallelism and even the blurring of the pause-sequence—presumably, the existence of one lineating system allows the loosening of another."[61] Murphy observes that "the alphabetic psalms generally consist of simple petitions and lessons."[62]

Psalm 119 reads like a diary entry—it is like reading someone's diary or spiritual journal. The Psalmist speaks of his walk with the Lord in this psalm. It is really a prayer. Nearly every verse in this psalm contains the term "law" or a synonym for it.[63] This psalm teaches that genuine godliness is marked by a love for and a delight in the Word of God. As the Psalmist composed this acrostic, I imagine he

---

[60] Kirkpatrick, *Psalms*, 693.

[61] Kugel, *The Idea of Biblical Poetry*, 311

[62] J. G. Murphy, *Psalms*, 189

[63] Exceptions are vv. 90, 121, 122, and 132.

might have thought, "What observation on my walk with God can I express in a sentence that begins with this letter?" "How can I pick up on the thought of the previous verse with another word of this letter?" For the most part, there is considerable variation in the initial words for each acrostic letter. This not only adds to the poetic beauty of the acrostic, but also creates a nice mixture of thought, ensuring that a variety of spiritual truths are expressed.

This psalm sounds very much like the prayer of a young man, and especially of that young man David (cf. vv. 9, 46, 67, 99). This is a man who has completed the initial stage of growth as an adult believer, and who is now looking forward to a life of service to God. He loves Yahweh with all his heart, and meditates continually on His word, yet he continues to struggle with sin and temptation (vv. 37, 115, 136). His faith is vibrant and passionate, and he is blessed by God, yet he is still pressured by enemies (vv. 68, 139, 153, 157, 170).

# Psalm 120

**Subject:** Prayer for deliverance from deceitful, violent men
**Author:** Not stated; however, it is probable, on the basis of vv. 6-7, that this is a Davidic Psalm. David was known in his lifetime as a man of war, but he was really a man of peace at heart who simply was attacked often. Compare also Ps 120:1 with Ps 18:6 (Davidic), and Ps 120:3-6 with Ps 57:4 (Davidic).

**Outline**
   I.  Yahweh's past deliverances recalled v. 1
  II.  Prayer for deliverance from lying lips v. 2
 III.  The reward of the deceitful tongue vv. 3-4
 IV.  Complaint regarding oppression vv. 5-7

Psalm 120 is the first of the songs of ascents, which are collected into a single unit in the Psalter (Pss 120–134). Most of the songs of ascents are very short. This indicates that they were sung as the Levites processed up the steps of the temple. The only one of these Psalms that is longer is 132, and that is because it was written for the dedication of the temple. The Songs of Ascents were largely composed before the exile, but their titles and associated usage could have been created after the exile. The collection itself was made after the exile.

# Psalm 121

**Subject:** Yahweh, the sole source of the Psalmist's help, unfailingly watches over and protects His own
**Author:** Not stated, but probably David in view of the similarity between Psalm 121:2 and Psalm 124:8 (Davidic). The subject matter of Psalm 121 is similar to Psalm 91, which is unsigned.

**Outline**
   I.  Yahweh the sole source of the Psalmist's help vv. 1-2
  II.  Yahweh's keeping actions vv. 3-8
      A.  Yahweh's constant watching vv. 3-4
      B.  Yahweh's constant sheltering vv. 5-6
      C.  Yahweh's constant safekeeping vv. 7-8

# Psalm 122

**Subject:** David describes his admiration for Jerusalem and for the house of Yahweh, and prays for the peace and wellness of Jerusalem

**Author:** David; note that the tabernacle is sometimes called the house of Yahweh, as is the tent which David pitched for the ark of the covenant. In 2 Samuel 12:20, it is said that David went into the house of Yahweh (cf. 1 Chr 22:1; Ps 23:6; 27:4).

**Outline**
I. David's joy in going to Yahweh's house v. 1
II. David's wonder and admiration for Jerusalem vv. 2-5
III. Prayer for the peace of Jerusalem vv. 6-8
IV. Vow to seek the good of Jerusalem v. 9

# Psalm 123

**Subject:** An expectant prayer for Yahweh's mercy upon His despised people
**Author:** not stated

**Outline**
I. The expectation of mercy from Yahweh vv. 1-2
II. The plea for mercy and its reason vv. 3-4

# Psalm 124

**Subject:** Yahweh's deliverance of His people from what would have been certain destruction is recalled and celebrated
**Author:** David

**Outline**
I. The threat of destruction recalled vv. 1-5
II. Yahweh praised for rescuing His people vv. 6-8

# Psalm 125

**Subject:** A celebration of Yahweh's care for His people
**Author:** not stated

**Outline**
I. The situation of Yahweh's people compared to Mount Zion vv. 1-3
II. Yahweh's treatment of the good contrasted with His treatment of the crooked vv. 4-5

# Psalm 126

**Subject:** A thanksgiving to Yahweh for the return from exile, and a prayer for renewed prosperity in the land
**Author:** not stated

**Outline**
  I.   The glad return to Zion recounted vv. 1-2
 II.   Yahweh praised for the return and entreated for renewed prosperity vv. 3-4
III.   The hope of restoration expressed vv. 5-6

This psalm was likely written when the foundation of the temple was finished in Ezra 2. On that occasion, some cried, but the laying of a new foundation was an act of sowing which anticipated complete restoration.
This may well be the latest Psalm in the Psalter.

# Psalm 127

**Subject:** A didactic psalm which teaches that Yahweh is the Protector and Builder of every man's house
**Author:** Solomon

**Outline**
  I.   The futility of man's efforts to build and protect vv. 1-2
 II.   The gift of children from Yahweh vv. 3-5

# Psalm 128

**Subject:** A description of the blessedness of the man who fears Yahweh, and a pronouncement of blessing upon the God-fearing hearer
**Author:** not stated

**Outline**
  I.   The blessedness of the man who fears Yahweh vv. 1-4
 II.   The blessing pronounced vv. 5-6

# Psalm 129

**Subject:** Yahweh's past deliverances from affliction recalled as a basis for the prayer for the overthrow of Zion's current and future enemies
**Author:** Not stated, but probably David in view of the parallels between Psalm 129:1b and Psalm 124:1b (Davidic), between Psalm 129:3 and Psalm 141:7 (Davidic), and between Psalm 129:6 and Psalm 37:2 (Davidic).

**Outline**
  I.   Remembrance of Yahweh's past deliverances from affliction vv. 1-4
 II.   Prayer for the overthrow of Zion's enemies vv. 5-8

# Psalm 130

**Subject:** The Psalmist expresses confidence that Yahweh will hear his cry because He forgives iniquities, and exhorts Israel to place their hope in Yahweh in like manner
**Author:** not stated

**Outline**
I. The Psalmist's call to Yahweh vv. 1-2
II. The Psalmist's hope in forgiveness vv. 3-4
III. The Psalmist's expectant waiting vv. 5-6
IV. The exhortation to Israel vv. 7-8

# Psalm 131

**Subject:** David's childlike trust in Yahweh given as a basis for Israel to hope in Yahweh
**Author:** David

**Outline**
I. David's renunciation of self-confidence v. 1
II. David's ease due to his confidence in Yahweh v. 2
III. Exhortation to Israel v. 3

# Psalm 132

**Subject:** A prayer for the dedication of Solomon's temple, and Yahweh's promise of blessing in response
**Author:** Not stated, but must be Solomon

The occasion for the psalm appears to be the dedication of Solomon's temple, and much of the language used is similar to that used by Solomon. Compare the following:

| **Psalm 132:4** | **Proverbs 6:4** |
|---|---|
| *I will not give sleep to mine eyes,* <br> *Or slumber to mine eyelids;* | *Give not sleep to thine eyes,* <br> *Nor slumber to thine eyelids:* |
| **Psalm 132:8-10** | **2 Chronicles 6:41-42** |
| *Arise, O Jehovah, into thy resting-place;* <br> *Thou, and the ark of thy strength.* <br> *Let thy priests be clothed with righteousness;* <br> *And let thy saints shout for joy.* <br> *For thy servant David's sake* <br> *Turn not away the face of thine anointed.* | *Now therefore arise, O Jehovah God, into thy resting-place, thou, and the ark of thy strength: let thy priests, O Jehovah God, be clothed with salvation, and let thy saints rejoice in goodness. O Jehovah God, turn not away the face of thine anointed: remember thy lovingkindness to David thy servant.* |

| Psalm 132:11-12 | 2 Chronicles 6:16 |
|---|---|
| *Jehovah hath sworn unto David in truth;*<br>*He will not turn from it:*<br>*Of the fruit of thy body will I set upon thy throne.*<br>*If thy children will keep my covenant*<br>*And my testimony that I will teach them,*<br>*Their children also shall sit upon thy throne for evermore.* | *Now therefore, O Jehovah, the God of Israel, keep with thy servant David my father that which thou hast promised him, saying, There shall not fail thee a man in my sight to sit on the throne of Israel, if only thy children take heed to their way, to walk in my law as thou hast walked before me.* |
| Psalm 132:14 | 1 Kings 8:13 |
| *This is my resting-place for ever:*<br>*Here will I dwell; for I have desired it.* | *I have surely built thee a house of habitation, a place for thee to dwell in for ever.* |
| Psalm 132:16 | 2 Chronicles 6:41b |
| *Her priests also will I clothe with salvation;*<br>*And her saints shall shout aloud for joy.* | *let thy priests, O Jehovah God, be clothed with salvation, and let thy saints rejoice in goodness.* |
| Psalm 132:17-18 | 1 Kings 2:33 |
| *There will I make the horn of David to bud:*<br>*I have ordained a lamp for mine anointed.*<br>*His enemies will I clothe with shame;*<br>*But upon himself shall his crown flourish.* | *unto David, and unto his seed, and unto his house, and unto his throne, shall there be peace for ever from Jehovah.* |

Probably Solomon's personal references to "David my father" are removed in this psalm because the choir of priests and Levites were to sing this song as the ark was carried into the temple.

**Outline**
  I.  Prayer to dedicate the temple vv. 1-10
      A. David's zeal for the house of Yahweh remembered vv. 1-5
      B. Response: the people assembling to worship vv. 6-7
      C. Call for Yahweh to inhabit the temple and bless His servants vv. 8-10
  II.  Yahweh's promise of blessing vv. 11-18
      A. Promise of blessing upon David vv. 11-12
      B. Promise of blessing upon Zion vv. 13-18

---

# Psalm 133

**Subject:** A celebration of the excellence of unity among believers
**Author:** David

**Outline**
  I.  The admiration of brotherly unity v. 1
  II.  Metaphors for brotherly unity vv. 2-3

---

# Psalm 134

**Subject:** The night watchmen in the temple called to bless Yahweh, with a blessing pronounced in response
**Author:** not stated

**Outline**
  I.  Call for the night watchmen to bless Yahweh vv. 1-2
  II.  Blessing pronounced in response v. 3

This psalm was likely used as a night greeting. It is a fitting conclusion to the fifteen songs of ascents.

# Psalm 135

**Subject:** Israel called to praise Yahweh because of His mighty acts on their behalf, in contrast to the non-action of the gods of the nations, to the ruin of their worshippers
**Author:** not stated

**Outline**
  I.  Call to praise Yahweh vv. 1-3
  II.  Yahweh's mighty acts on behalf of Israel recounted vv. 4-14
  III.  The impotence of the idols of the nations and their worshippers vv. 15-18
  IV.  Benediction: Israel called to bless Yahweh vv. 19-21

# Psalm 136

**Subject:** Yahweh praised for His everlasting lovingkindness, as demonstrated by the great wonders He has shown in creation, by the Exodus and Conquest, and by the daily grace given to His people and to all the world
**Author:** not stated

**Outline**
  I.  Call to give thanks to Yahweh vv. 1-4
  II.  Yahweh praised for His creative acts vv. 5-9
  III.  Yahweh praised for His deliverance of Israel from Egypt to Canaan vv. 10-22
  IV.  Yahweh praised for His continuing grace to Israel and to all flesh vv. 23-25
  V.  Concluding doxology v. 26

The repetition in this psalm is striking and tends to reinforce the point rather than becoming dull routine because this is the only place in the Psalter where it occurs. This psalm was designed for antiphonal singing, and is still sung antiphonally in Jewish synagogues to this day. The chorus "Give thanks to Yahweh of hosts, for Yahweh is good, for his lovingkindness endureth for ever" was the centerpiece of Israelite liturgy in the OT, similar to the Gloria Patri in the traditional liturgy of English-speaking churches. It occurs frequently in the OT as the refrain of the official temple choir (1 Chr 16:41; 2 Chr 5:13; 7:6; 20:21; Ezra 3:11; Jer 33:11; cf. 1 Chr 16:34; 2 Chr 7:3; Pss 100:5; 107:1; 118:1-4, 29).

It is likely that when this psalm was sung, the Levitical choir sang the first verse, and then the second half of each subsequent verse, with the people singing the first half of each verse (or vice versa).

# Psalm 137

**Subject:** Remembrance of Zion in the midst of the sorrows of exile

**Author:** Not stated; the Psalmist(s) was evidently a temple musician in Jerusalem before he was taken to Babylon

**Outline**
   I. The inability to sing in captivity vv. 1-3
  II. The refusal to sing in captivity vv. 4-6
 III. The prayer for vengeance in behalf of Jerusalem vv. 7-9

This psalm is a good example of later songwriting, as it was composed over four hundred years after David and Solomon. The more frequent use of אֵת is a characteristic of later songs. In addition, there are several places in this psalm where colon divisions are difficult to recognize.

---

# Psalm 138

**Subject:** A reflection on Yahweh's past and future goodness to David and to all men by means of His faithfulness to His Word
**Author:** David

**Outline**
   I. David's praise for Yahweh's faithfulness to him vv. 1-3
  II. Yahweh's praise from the kings of the earth vv. 4-6
 III. Yahweh's future faithfulness to David celebrated vv. 7-8

---

# Psalm 139

**Subject:** God's total knowledge of, presence with, and sovereignty over David is recounted as a source of confidence in God's care for David, in a just judgment of his wicked enemies, and in the correction of David's remaining personal faults
**Author:** David

**Outline**
   I. Yahweh's omniscience over David vv. 1-5
  II. Yahweh's omnipresence over David vv. 7-12
 III. Yahweh's sovereignty over David vv. 13-16
  IV. David's confidence in God's care vv. 17-18
   V. David's confidence in God's judgment of his wicked enemies vv. 19-22
  VI. David's request for God's identification and correction of his faults vv. 23-24

---

# Psalm 140

**Subject:** David confidently prays for Yahweh to protect him from the assaults of the wicked and to justly repay them for their deeds, in order to vindicate David's trust in Yahweh
**Author:** David

**Outline**
   I. Prayer for preservation from the violent vv. 1-5
  II. Prayer for the vindication of David's confidence in Yahweh vv. 6-8
 III. Prayer for the just retribution of the wicked vv. 9-11
  IV. Expression of confidence in Yahweh's deliverance vv. 12-13

# Psalm 141

**Subject:** David cries out to Yahweh in the midst of trouble, praying that he might remain separate from the wicked and be delivered from their assaults
**Author:** David

**Outline**
   I. The appeal for Yahweh to hear David's cry vv. 1-2
  II. The prayer to remain separate from the wicked vv. 3-6
 III. The prayer for deliverance from the assault of the wicked vv. 7-10

# Psalm 142

**Subject:** David's urgent but confident entreaty to Yahweh for deliverance at a time when all men had abandoned him and his enemies encompassed him
**Author:** David

**Outline**
   I. David's call to Yahweh vv. 1-2
  II. The exclusivity of David's hope in Yahweh vv. 3-5
 III. David's entreaty for deliverance from his persecutors vv. 6-7

# Psalm 143

**Subject:** An appeal for Yahweh to quickly deliver David from an enemy, and to revive his spirit
**Author:** David

**Outline**
   I. David's complaint vv. 1-6
      A. Appeal to Yahweh vv. 1-2
      B. The reason for the prayer: oppression by an enemy vv. 3-4
      C. The recollection of Yahweh's works vv. 5-6
  II. David's prayer for deliverance and revival vv. 7-12
      A. Prayer for Yahweh to manifest Himself to David vv. 7-8
      B. Prayer for the vindication of David's trust in Yahweh vv. 9-10
      C. Anticipation of deliverance and revival vv. 11-12

# Psalm 144

**Subject:** King David blesses Yahweh for His goodness to him, then prays for His coming in deliverance, praises Yahweh in anticipation of deliverance, and extols the happy state of Israel under Yahweh's care

**Author:** David

**Outline**

    I. Yahweh blessed for his goodness to David in spite of man's insignificance vv. 1-4

    II. Appeal for Yahweh to come and deliver David vv. 5-8

    III. David's praise for anticipated deliverance vv. 9-11

    IV. The blessedness of Yahweh's delivered people extolled vv. 12-15

# Psalm 145

**Subject:** Yahweh extolled for His universal wondrous works, His graciousness, the glory of His kingdom, and His preserving and sustaining grace

**Author:** David

**Outline**

    I. Resolve to extol Yahweh vv. 1-3

    II. Declaration of Yahweh's works vv. 4-7

    III. Declaration of Yahweh's graciousness vv. 8-9

    IV. Yahweh's glorious kingdom extolled vv. 10-13

    V. Yahweh's preserving grace to all flesh vv. 14-17

    VI. Yahweh's graciousness to the righteous vv. 18-20

    VII. Call to praise Yahweh v. 21

Psalm 145 is an acrostic in which each verse begins with a successive letter of the Hebrew alphabet. There is no נ (*nûn*) verse in the Masoretic Text (*nûn* is skipped between v. 13 and v. 14), but this is in keeping with the variation in form that is found in the other biblical acrostics.

# Psalm 146

**Subject:** Yahweh praised as the one true Helper

**Author:** not stated

**Outline**

    I. Call to praise Yahweh vv. 1-2

    II. The folly of trusting in man vv. 3-4

    III. The wisdom of trusting in Yahweh vv. 5-7b

    IV. Yahweh magnified for His saving power vv. 7b-10

This is a beautiful psalm, both in its language and in the instruction contained therein. It is the first of the five Hallelujah Psalms which close the Psalter.

Some suggest that there are enough verbal parallels between Psalm 145 and Psalm 146 that they must have been written by the same author. If this is the case, then the author of Psalm 146 is David. Also compare Psalm 146:5 with Psalm 124:8 (Davidic).

# Psalm 147

**Subject:** Call to praise Yahweh for His boundless power and goodness, by which he has lifted up His people and conferred special blessing upon them

**Author:** not stated

## Outline
I. Call to praise Yahweh for building up His people by His great power vv. 1-6
II. Call to praise Yahweh for His providential goodness vv. 7-11
III. Call for Israel to praise Yahweh as the recipients of His special favor vv. 12-20

# Psalm 148

**Subject:** All of creation invoked to praise Yahweh
**Author:** not stated

## Outline
I. Call to praise Yahweh v. 1a
II. Call for the heavenlies to praise Yahweh vv. 1b-6
III. Call for the earthlies to praise Yahweh vv. 7-14c
IV. Call to praise Yahweh v. 14d

# Psalm 149

**Subject:** An exhortation to the saints to praise Yahweh for saving them and giving them the honor of executing judgment upon the nations

**Author:** not stated

## Outline
I. Call to praise Yahweh for His salvation of His people vv. 1-4
II. Call to praise Yahweh for giving judgment to His saints vv. 5-8

# Psalm 150

**Subject:** A call for all the living to praise Yahweh for who He is and what He has done, with all kinds of musical instruments

**Author:** not stated

## Outline
I. Call to praise Yahweh where He is v. 1

II. Call to praise Yahweh for what He has done v. 2a
III. Call to praise Yahweh for who He is v. 2b
IV. Call to praise Yahweh with all kinds of instruments vv. 3-5
V. Call for all the living to praise Yahweh v. 6

This is the closing doxology to the Psalter. There is no other psalm that could close the Psalter so fittingly as this one. It is a brief, yet pointed and all-encompassing call to praise Yahweh, which is the aim of the entire Psalter.

## Bibliography for the Psalms

There are an enormous number of commentaries on the Psalms, far more than for any other book of the OT. Many of the commentaries published since the early 20th century are critical, and many only deal with certain portions of the Psalter. Many newer evangelical works are using form criticism. The following bibliography should be regarded as preliminary.

Two excellent commentaries on the Psalms are the *Speaker's Commentary* (Cook, Elliot, Johnson) and Murphy. Others: Barnes, Kirkpatrick, Delitzsch, Perowne, Plumer, Forbes. The *Speaker's Commentary* takes the most theologically conservative approach to the Psalms, including the messianic Psalms. It has some of the most lucid comments on the Psalms, and may be the best all-around commentary. The *Trinity Psalter* can be surprisingly helpful as an interpretational aid. One value in using nineteenth century commentaries on the Psalms is that most do not use form-critical terminology or employ critical methods of analysis.

Alexander, Joseph Addison. *The Psalms Translated and Explained*. Reprint: Grand Rapids: Baker, 1975.
**Note:** Originally published ca. 1850.

Allen, Leslie C. *Psalms 101–150*. Word Biblical Commentary, vol. 21. Waco, TX: Word Books, 1983.

Alter, Robert. *The Book of Psalms: A Translation with Commentary*. New York: W. W. Norton, 2007.

Anderson, A. A. *Psalms 1–72*. Volume 1 of *The Book of Psalms*. New Century Bible Commentary. Grand Rapids: Eerdmans, 1972.

————. *Psalms 73–150*. Volume 2 of *The Book of Psalms*. New Century Bible Commentary. Grand Rapids: Eerdmans, 1972.

Barnes, Albert. *Psalms*. 3 vols. Notes on the Old Testament: Explanatory and Practical. Edited by Robert Frew. Reprint: Grand Rapids: Baker, 1950.
**Note:** Volume 1 covers Pss 1–41; vol. 2 covers Pss 42–89; vol. 3 covers Pss 90–150. This was the final commentary which Barnes produced before his death as an old man.

Blaising, Craig A., Carmen S. Hardin, and Thomas C. Oden, eds. *Psalms 1–50*. Ancient Christian Commentary on Scripture: Old Testament, vol. 7. Downers Grove, IL: InterVarsity Press, 2008.

Boice, James Montgomery. *Psalms 1–41*. Volume 1 of *Psalms*. Grand Rapids: Baker, 1994.

————. *Psalms 107–150*. Volume 3 of *Psalms*. Grand Rapids: Baker, 1998.

Cole, Robert. "The Composition of the Psalter and the Folly of Form Criticism." Paper presented at the annual meeting of the ETS. New Orleans, LA, Nov 19, 2009.
**Note:** This was an excellent paper.

Cook, F. C., G. H. S. Johnson, and C. J. Elliot. "Psalms." In *The Holy Bible with an Explanatory and Critical Commentary*, ed. F. C. Cook, vol. 4, 146-512. Cambridge: C. J. Clay, 1892.
**Note:** Cook wrote the Introduction and the commentary on Pss 1, 3–7, 9–22, 24–28, 30–64, 66–67, 69–76, and 78–89. Elliot wrote the commentary on Pss 91–99 and 141–150 and the Excursus upon Pss 91–100. Johnson wrote the commentary on Pss 2, 8, 23, 29, 65, 68, 77, 90, and 100–140.

Craigie, Peter C. with a supplement by Marvin E. Tate. *Psalms 1–50*. 2nd ed. Word Biblical Commentary, vol. 19. Thomas Nelson, 2004.

Dahood, Mitchell. *Psalms I: 1–50*. Anchor Bible. Garden City, NY: Doubleday & Company, 1965.

———. *Psalms II: 51–100*. Anchor Bible. Garden City, NY: Doubleday & Company, 1968.

———. *Psalms III: 101–150*. Anchor Bible. Garden City, NY: Doubleday & Company, 1970.

Delitzsch, Franz. *Biblical Commentary on the Psalms*. Translated by Francis Bolton. 3 vols. Biblical Commentary on the Old Testament. Reprint: Grand Rapids: Eerdmans, 1949–52.
**Note:** Volume 1 covers Pss 1–35; vol. 2 covers Pss 36–83; vol. 3 covers Pss 84–150.

Forbes, John. *Studies on the Book of Psalms: The Structural Connection of the Book of Psalms, Both in Single Psalms and in the Psalter as an Organic Whole*. Edited by James Forrest. Edinburgh: T. & T. Clark, 1888.
**Note:** Robert Cole regards John Forbes as an important but neglected nineteenth century Psalms commentator who deals extensively with the canonical structure of the Psalms.

Futato, Mark D. "The Book of Psalms." Pages 1-450 in *Cornerstone Biblical Commentary*, ed. Philip W. Comfort. Carol Stream, IL: Tyndale House, 2009.

Gaebelein, Arno C. *The Book of Psalms: A Devotional and Prophetic Commentary*. Neptune, NJ: Loizeaux Brothers, 1939.

Goldingay, John. *Psalms 1–41*. Volume 1 of *Psalms*. Baker Commentary on the Old Testament Wisdom and Psalms, ed. Tremper Longman III. Grand Rapids: Baker, 2006.

———. *Psalms 42–89*. Volume 2 of *Psalms*. Baker Commentary on the Old Testament Wisdom and Psalms, ed. Tremper Longman III. Grand Rapids: Baker, 2007.

———. *Psalms 90–150*. Volume 3 of *Psalms*. Baker Commentary on the Old Testament Wisdom and Psalms, ed. Tremper Longman III. Grand Rapids: Baker, 2008.

Gunkel, Hermann and Joachim Begrich. *Introduction to the Psalms: The Genres of the Religious Lyric of Israel*. Translated by James D. Nogalski. Mercer Library of Biblical Studies. Macon, GA: Mercer, 1998.
**Note:** Gunkel is a German liberal who developed the form critical study of the Psalms.

Harman, Allan M. *Commentary on the Psalms*. Mentor. Fearn, Ross-shire, Great Britain. Christian Focus, 1998.

Hossfeld, Frank-Lothar and Erich Zenger. *A Commentary on Psalms 51–100*. Klaus Baltzer, ed. Linda M. Maloney, trans. Hermeneia. Minneapolis: Fortress Press, 2005.

Keller, Philip. *A Shepherd Looks at Psalm 23*. Grand Rapids: Zondervan, 1970.

Kidner, Derek. *Psalms 1–72: An Introduction and Commentary on Books I and II of the Psalms*. Tyndale Old Testament Commentaries. Downers Grove, IL: Inter-Varsity Press, 1973.

————. *Psalms 73–150: An Introduction and Commentary on Books III–V of the Psalms*. Tyndale Old Testament Commentaries. Downers Grove, IL: Inter-Varsity Press, 1975.

Kirkpatrick, A. F. *The Book of Psalms*. Cambridge Bible for Schools and Colleges. Cambridge: Cambridge, 1902
**Note:** Kirkpatrick is in some ways an excellent commentator, but he often takes a liberal view of the background of psalms, especially prophetic or messianic psalms. Overall, though, this is among the best commentaries on Psalms that I have used. Kirkpatrick is obviously very intelligent and knowledgeable, though he is not as conservative as one would like.

Kraus, Hans-Joachim. *Psalms 1–59*. Translated by Hilton C. Oswald. A Continental Commentary. Minneapolis: Fortress Press, 1993.

————. *Psalms 60–150*. Translated by Hilton C. Oswald. A Continental Commentary. Minneapolis: Fortress Press, 1993.

Kugel, James. *The Idea of Biblical Poetry: Parallelism and Its History*. Baltimore: Johns Hopkins UP, 1981.

Hengstenberg, E. W. *Commentary on the Psalms*. 4th ed. 3 vols. Edinburgh: T. & T. Clark, 1869.

Leupold, H. C. *Exposition of the Psalms*. Grand Rapids: Baker, 1959.

MacLaren, Alexander. *Psalms I.—XXXVIII*. Volume 1 of *The Psalms*. The Expositor's Bible, ed. W. Robertson Nicoll. London: Hodder and Stoughton, 1893.

————. *Psalms XXXIX.—LXXXIX*. Volume 2 of *The Psalms*. The Expositor's Bible, ed. W. Robertson Nicoll. London: Hodder and Stoughton, 1893.

————. *Psalms XC.—CL*. Volume 3 of *The Psalms*. The Expositor's Bible, ed. W. Robertson Nicoll. London: Hodder and Stoughton, 1894.

Meyer, F. B. *Gems from the Psalms*. Westchester, IL: Good News Publishers, 1976.
**Note:** This book has also been published under other titles.

Mowinckel, Sigmund. *The Psalms in Israel's Worship*. Translated by D. R. Ap-Thomas. Grand Rapids: Eerdmans, 2004.
**Note:** The first edition was published in 1962. This is two volumes in one. Mowinckel's work is an influential liberal expansion of Gunkel's.

Murphy, James G. *A Critical and Exegetical Commentary on the Book of Psalms with a New Translation*. Andover: Warren Draper, 1876.
**Note:** Murphy's commentary is excellent. He is very conservative, his commentary on the text is helpful, and he has helpful notes on the Hebrew text and translation.

Perowne, J. J. Stewart. *Psalms 1–72*. Volume 1 of *The Book of Psalms: A New Translation with Introductions and Notes Explanatory and Critical*. 4th ed. George Bell and Sons, 1878. Reprint: Grand Rapids: Zondervan, 1966.

———. *Psalms 73–150*. Volume 2 of *The Book of Psalms: A New Translation with Introductions and Notes Explanatory and Critical*. 4th ed. George Bell and Sons, 1878. Reprint: Grand Rapids: Zondervan, 1966.

Phillips, John. *Psalms 1–88*. Exploring the Psalms. Neptune, NJ: Loizeaux Brothers, 1988.

———. *Psalms 89–150*. Exploring the Psalms. Neptune, NJ: Loizeaux Brothers, 1988.

Plumer, William S. *Psalms: A Critical and Expository Commentary with Doctrinal and Practical Remarks*. Reprint: Edinburgh: Banner of Truth Trust, 1975.
**Note:** Originally published in 1867.

Ross, Allen P. "Psalms." Pages 779-899 in *The Bible Knowledge Commentary: Old Testament*, ed. John F. Walvoord and Roy B. Zuck. Colorado Springs: Chariot Victor, 1985.

Scroggie, W. Graham. *Psalms I to L*. Rev. ed. Volume 1 of *The Psalms*. Know Your Bible. London: Pickering & Inglis, 1948.

———. *Psalms LI to C*. Rev. ed. Volume 2 of *The Psalms*. Know Your Bible. London: Pickering & Inglis, 1949.

———. *Psalms CI to CXXIV*. Volume 3 of *The Psalms*. Know Your Bible. London: Pickering & Inglis, 1950.

———. *Psalms CXXXV to CL*. Volume 4 of *The Psalms*. Know Your Bible. London: Pickering & Inglis, 1951.

Spurgeon, C. H. *Psalm I to LVII*. Volume 1 of *The Treasury of David*. Reprint: Peabody, MA: Hendrickson, 1990.

———. *Psalm LVIII to CX*. Volume 2 of *The Treasury of David*. Reprint: Peabody, MA: Hendrickson, 1990.

———. *Psalm CXI to CL*. Volume 3 of *The Treasury of David*. Reprint: Peabody, MA: Hendrickson, 1990.

Tate, Marvin E. *Psalms 51–100*. Word Biblical Commentary, vol. 20. Nashville: Thomas Nelson, 1990.

*Trinity Psalter: Music Edition*. Pittsburgh: Crown & Covenant Publications, 2000.

VanGemeren, Willem A. "Psalms." Pages 3-880 in *The Expositor's Bible Commentary*, vol. 5. Grand Rapids: Zondervan, 1991.

———. "Psalms." Pages 21-1011 in *The Expositor's Bible Commentary: Revised Edition*, vol. 5. Grand Rapids: Zondervan, 2008.

Waltner, James H. *Psalms*. Believers Church Bible Commentary. Scottdale, PA: Herald Press, 2006.

Westermann, Claus. *The Living Psalms*. Translated by J. R. Porter. Grand Rapids: Eerdmans, 1989.

Wesselschmidt, Quentin F. and Thomas C. Oden, eds. *Psalms 51–150*. Ancient Christian Commentary on Scripture: Old Testament, vol. 8. Downers Grove, IL: InterVarsity Press, 2007.

Witvliet, John D. *The Biblical Psalms in Christian Worship: A Brief Introduction and Guide to Resources*. Grand Rapids: Eerdmans, 2007.

# Interpretive Guide to Proverbs

Although the entire Bible is a book of wisdom, Proverbs is the one book of the Bible whose central subject is wisdom. "A variety of terms, wisdom, knowledge, understanding, discretion, subtlety, are indeed employed, to set forth under different aspects the nature of the instruction to be given; but the one comprehensive word which includes them all is Wisdom."[1] The Hebrew word חָכְמָה (*wisdom*) has been defined in various ways by Christian commentators, but is not expressly defined in Scripture, except by the numerous parallel concepts which it encompasses, and by the things which characterize it. Wisdom encompasses many concepts and many applications to specific situations, which makes learning it a lifelong process; it involves one's total way of thinking and worldview.

For Solomon, wisdom is inseparably linked to the practice of true religion and the worship of the living God. The stated theme of the book in the prologue is that the fear of Yahweh (i.e., the belief in and proper devotion to God) is the starting point of the quest for wisdom, and the condition which necessarily accompanies its acquisition (1:7). This same principle is reaffirmed in the exhortation to the son to obtain wisdom (2:5-6), in the final call of wisdom at the end of the address to the son (9:10), and at the end of the book's capstone, as a summary of the worthy woman's character (31:30). Solomon makes no apology for linking his religion so explicitly to his practical instruction, and in fact asserts that any attempt to describe wise principles apart from deep personal piety toward the living God would be the height of folly. Religious themes are profuse throughout the Proverbs. Solomon exhorts his hearers to weave true religion into the fabric of everyday life in order to be wise, righteous, and blessed. The name יהוה (*Yahweh*) occurs some eighty-seven times in the book, including multiple instances in most chapters. Yahweh must be the central reality in the wise man's worldview. Many of the proverbs simply mention Yahweh's relation to man, with the assumption that the reader knows Yahweh and believes His Word. An entire paragraph in the address to the son exhorts him to serve and honor Yahweh (3:1-12), as do many individual proverbs. The proof of wisdom's worth is Yahweh's use of wisdom from before time began to bring the world into being (8:22-31). In the capstone of the book, the great sage Agur opens his speech with a statement of his commitment to fidelity to God and His Word (30:1b-9). While it would not be possible to mention Yahweh explicitly in every single proverb, fear of God is specifically stated to be the key to wisdom, and various aspects of God's relationship to man are spoken of frequently throughout the book. Solomon's absolute refusal to acknowledge the possibility of wisdom apart from fidelity to the one true God sets his wisdom apart from all other so-called "wisdom" of the ancient world. It also explains why the wise men of this world do not regard Solomon's writings as special, or even as worth reading—in spite of the fact that Solomon was the wisest man who ever lived (so 1 Kgs 3:12; 4:31; 10:23; 2 Chr 1:12). Since one cannot understand wisdom without an accurate knowledge of God and of His Word and a personal relationship with Him, the unsaved cannot recognize Solomon's wisdom for what it is.

The "wisdom literature" of ancient pagan cultures, by contrast, is really not wise. Much of it is self-serving, telling you how to get what you want in life; it is superstitious; it is polytheistic; it often attributes the bad things in life to demons; it calls on the influence of magic; and it is involved with cultic sensuality. Likewise, the intellectualism of the twenty-first century world is not true wisdom, for it is clear that the more the world develops technology the more it uses this technology to push back the limits of depravity, so that man is now in the process of destroying himself through his own devices. The world is more broken, unstable, and confused than ever before, and yet it continues to insist that one must separate his personal religious devotion from his studies in order to obtain objective truth—a philosophy which the book of Proverbs asserts is guaranteed to produce folly.

---

[1] T. T. Perowne, *The Proverbs: With Introduction and Notes* (Cambridge Bible for Schools and Colleges; Cambridge: Cambridge, 1899), 9.

Much of Solomon's wisdom was developed simply by careful reflection on things which he saw and experienced (cf. Prov 16:23; 24:30-34). One who thoughtfully analyzes everything that happens and learns from it will become wise over time, even with limited experiences, for it is possible, through keen observation, to garner momentous lessons from seemingly insignificant experiences. When Solomon saw the most ordinary things in life, he pondered them deeply, and they became metaphors and object lessons: "This is like that" (cf. Prov 11:22; 17:12; 19:13; 21:9, 19; 25:19; 26:17, etc.). Solomon did not have to see everything to learn about everything, nor did he need to read handbooks and manuals. When he saw ants in his courtyard, he learned a profound lesson about hard work, and a walk past an overgrown vineyard produced the same effect.

In Solomon's case, one would suppose that his life experiences must have been very limited, and far removed from the hard realities of human existence. He was born and raised in a king's palace, and simply inherited an empire that had been won for him by his father. Throughout his long and peaceful reign, he possessed more wealth and power than anyone else on earth. Yet his writings are firmly connected to reality, and are imbued with a strong sense of the hardships and injustices of life. If it were not for the biographical information recorded about the author, the reader of Proverbs might think the book was composed by a poor man who had suffered much in life. The vastness of Solomon's understanding of life apparently grew out of his rather limited window on the world as prince and king. He was able to lean from every experience, and to extrapolate much concerning the ways of people and the nature of life. Solomon's example proves that one ultimately does not have to experience or read everything to be wise, but only to reflect on the things he does see and experience. That said, broad and varied experiences are usually eye-openers, and wise men tend to be experience-gatherers.

So, do you want to be wise? Then carefully observe ordinary life and deeply ponder it, rather than living by event and instinct like everyone else. Of course, gaining wisdom is a lifelong process, and the one who properly seeks wisdom will become wiser and more mature as he grows older.

The proverbs express timeless, universal truth, and are as relevant today in America as they were in ancient Israel. They do not so much argue for truth as present it and allow it commend itself to the man who has a heart of wisdom. The proverbs are practical truths, about the nuts and bolts of how to live life, and yet are philosophical at the same time.

Some of the proverbs are not prescriptive (*Do this!*), but observational (*This is the way things are*—cf. 10:15; 21:9; 27:8, 14). The intent of the observational (descriptive) proverbs is to move the reader to act in light of the observations noted, or just to improve the reader's understanding of life. Many of the insights and observations are seemingly obvious ones, yet very often, if we do not read or hear the obvious, we do not think about it on our own, and ultimately we do not apply common sense in our daily decisions. A man who studies the Proverbs is likely to have the right sayings come to mind at critical moments as he goes about his daily business.

Many of the proverbs are statements of general regularities and not hard-and-fast rules, though some are. However, this is no different than commands and observations in the rest of Scripture. When Peter says, "Be subject to every human institution for the Lord's sake" (1 Pet 2:13), it is understood that this is a generally applicable rule. It would be unnecessarily pedantic for Peter to write, "Be subject to every human institution for the Lord's sake, except if the king tells you to worship an idol, in which case you have an obligation to obey God rather than man." Common sense is needed when interpreting the Bible. There is no need to make the simple complex by introducing theories about genre, or by claiming that the exceptions negate the literal meaning of the text.

Proverbs is frequently quoted by the NT writers, "who considered it as a treasure of revealed morality, whence Christians were to derive their rules of conduct."[2] Thus, the whole of this book is applicable to believers today; it was not just for the dispensation of the Law. Proverbs does contain a theme of temporal reward for right living—if you live wisely, you will be blessed, whereas if you live

---

[2] Thomas Hartwell Horne, *An Introduction to the Critical Study and Knowledge of the Holy Scriptures* (9th ed.; London: Longman, Brown, Green, and Longmans, 1846), 4:119.

foolishly, you will suffer for it—but so does the NT (cf. 1 Pet 3:10-17). There were exceptions both then and now (cf. Ps 73), but in the end it is better for the righteous (cf. Eccl 8:12-13).

Proverbs is a vital book to understand, because without wisdom it is impossible to live a life that is pleasing to God or that is successful in the true sense of that term. Proverbs is a book that fathers ought to teach their sons from an early age to start them down the right path in life (cf. 4:1-9). It is a book that pastors should teach their congregations, and it is a book that laymen should study on their own. It is a book that ought to be a focus of academic study by Christian scholars who write to a specifically Christian audience with the aim of edifying the church (as opposed to those who write to a general academic audience, with an aim to participate in the mainstream academic discussion that is dominated by critical scholars). It is vital for the man of God to master the art of living. He must understand and apply common sense; he must learn how to handle the practical, ordinary issues of life. Many ministers and laymen alike have been ruined through a lack of practical wisdom.

It is ironic that the three books of Proverbs, Ecclesiastes, and Song of Songs, which preserve the greatest words of wisdom from the wisest man who ever lived—words which were also inspired by God's Holy Spirit—are not recognized by secular scholars as being special in any way. They think that the wisdom of these books is mostly borrowed from or similar to the wisdom of the surrounding pagan cultures, and that Proverbs, Ecclesiastes, and Song of Songs were compiled or edited by Hebrew scribes long after the time of Solomon—whose very existence most deny. Even many conservative evangelical scholars and pastors deny the basic message of Ecclesiastes, despite its special place as the summary statement and culmination of all of Solomon's thought. The men who have the reputation for being the wisest in this age cannot recognize true wisdom when it is waved before their eyes, because it is a wisdom from above which is not understood by the natural man, nor apprehended by culturally-conditioned ways of thinking (cf. 1 Cor 2). The Queen of Sheba came from the ends of the earth to hear this wisdom, whereas modern man, who has free access to it, has no appreciation for it. It is not unlikely, based on Matt 12:42 and Luke 11:31, that the Queen of Sheba will stand up in the final day of judgment and condemn those who have brushed aside Solomon's wisdom.

Churches today have a huge number of programs for helping people with their marriages, with their finances, with addictions, and with any other problems they may be facing in life. Yet no church that I know of has a program to encourage its people to pursue wisdom. There are no "wisdom retreats," "wisdom seminars," or "wisdom fellowships." Pastors do not passionately call their congregations to make the search for wisdom the great priority of their lives, nor do they preach sermon series in which they work desperately to convince their people that wisdom is the most precious thing in life, the foremost thing they should be directing their time and energy to pursuing. Youth pastors do not challenge teenage boys to embark on the quest for wisdom. Yet it is a direct result of the depreciation of wisdom that there are so many other problems in the church, and that all of the programs that have been developed by the church have failed to mitigate these problems. If people understood the value of wisdom, they would give all that they had for it, yet wisdom is for the most part wholly neglected. People pursue money, relationships, and status instead. In fact, many of the church's popular programs are essentially designed to make life manageable while continuing to live by event and instinct, without embarking on a great quest for wisdom. It is our prayer that the church will make its priorities the priorities of this book of Proverbs.

## Author

The author of the book of Proverbs is clearly stated in the first verse: "Solomon the son of David, king of Israel." This heading covers the material in the book from 1:1 to 24:22. The heading in 24:23, "These also are [sayings] of the wise," could be read to indicate that 24:23-34 are non-Solomonic proverbs, although 24:33-34 is duplicated from 6:10-11. The use of the first person in these verses would also seem indicative of Solomonic authorship. Chapters 25–29 are prefaced by the heading, "These also are proverbs of Solomon, which the men of Hezekiah king of Judah copied out." Chapter 30 is said to be "the words of Agur the son of Jakeh; the oracle," or "the words of Agur the son of Jakeh, of Massa." Since Agur's oracle is written in Hebrew, and it is contained in the Hebrew Scriptures, and he was clearly a firm believer in the true God, he must have been closely associated with Israel in some way, if not actually an Israelite (compare Prov 30:5 with Ps 18:30). However, his oracle reveals that he was not a wealthy man (30:7-9), and thus not a king as is sometimes suggested. Chapter 31 is said to be "the words of King Lemuel; the oracle which his mother taught him," or "the words of Lemuel king of Massa, which his mother taught him." Massa was a north Arabian tribe (cf. Gen 25:14), which would have had contact with Israel and could have contained true believers. Since 31:10-31 is an acrostic poem, it seems that it must have been originally composed in Hebrew or a related Canaanite language. The languages of Ammon, Moab, and Edom were virtually identical with Hebrew, and it is possible that surrounding desert tribes may have spoken Canaanite as well. It may also be noted that Solomon did not follow the principles of ch. 31 in selecting a wife, and the use of Aramaic words in 31:2-3 is out of character for Hebrew writers.

Thus, Solomon was both the author and the writer of 1:1–24:22. Probably Solomon added 24:23-34 and chs. 30–31 as the conclusion to his work, while the Solomonic proverbs of chs. 25–29 were inserted during the national spiritual revival at the time of Hezekiah, probably under the direction of the prophet Isaiah. Solomon was the author of all but chs. 30–31, and the writer of all but chs. 25–29.

According to 1 Kgs 4:32, Solomon spoke 3,000 proverbs, of which only about one-sixth have been preserved in Scripture. The ones recorded in the books of Proverbs and Ecclesiastes are the best of the best, the ones ordered and inspired by the Spirit of God.

Solomon was the wisest man who ever lived, apart from the Lord Jesus Christ Himself (so 1 Kgs 3:12). Yet his wisdom, like all spiritual truth, is only recognizable by the spiritually attuned—by true believers. To the secular mind, Solomon's wisdom is no different from the pagan "wisdom" literature of the ancient world, and is not particularly helpful for contemporary life. In fact, liberal scholarly study of the Proverbs has focused on finding parallels with other literature of the ancient Near East in order to support their claim that the Bible is a non-unique, and largely borrowed, human product. In reality, there is little similarity between the proverbs and other ancient Near Eastern wisdom literature. Of course, the literary structure of Hebrew proverbs bears some similarity to literary structures used elsewhere in the Semitic world, but this is different from thought-borrowing. In addition, it seems that parallelism is the ideal form of elevated literary style, since it was used all the way back in Gen 4:23-24 and 9:25-27, before Hebrew existed as a language, and before the ancient Near Eastern cultures as we know them existed. It is possible that some of Solomon's proverbs were not original with him, such as "the fear of Yahweh is the beginning of knowledge" (cf. Job 28:28; Ps 111:10), but the non-original proverbs were adapted from other believers, not from pagan literature. It should also be noted that 1 Kgs 4:34 says that all peoples, from all the kingdoms of the earth, came to hear the wisdom of Solomon in his lifetime, and thus it would be expected that some of Solomon's wisdom would be preserved in some form in the writings of other ancient cultures.

According to 1 Kgs 4:33, Solomon had an extraordinary knowledge of biology, and presumably of other areas of science and mathematics as well. Yet the Bible does not preserve any of Solomon's scientific knowledge, though the world today would likely recognize its genius. From a biblical perspective, scientific wisdom is unimportant, impractical, and unimpressive in comparison with spiritual truth, for man's real need is spiritual, not physical.

## Date and Occasion of Writing

Solomon's first biblical compositions, the Song of Songs and Psalm 132, were written in his early years. Possibly Psalms 72 and 127 were as well. Solomon probably put this book of Proverbs in writing at a later point in his life, probably under prophetic instigation, in order to preserve his wisdom for future generations. The book of Proverbs was, however, in all probability written before Ecclesiastes (ca. 931 B.C.), which gives Solomon's final reflections on life as an old man. Perhaps Solomon wrote the book of

Proverbs around 940 B.C., in the thirtieth year of his reign—before constructing the high places for idolatrous worship—with Hezekiah's scribes inserting chs. 25–29 between the years 715 and 686 as part of the national spiritual revival which occurred during his reign.

## Purpose and Message

The stated purpose of the book of Proverbs is to instruct believers, especially young men, concerning wisdom and wise living (1:2-7). The specific instructions in the book are varied and multifaceted, but can be distilled into a single basic message. Wisdom is of inestimable value and is absolutely necessary to obtain: therefore give yourself entirely over to the fear of God and the pursuit of wisdom, for all those who seek wisdom in the fear of God will obtain it (1:7; 2:1-8; 9:10). The presupposition behind the message is also a dominant theme of the book: you need to find wisdom because everyone starts out ignorant and in grave danger of falling into life's snares, and will not find wisdom without an intentional, focused, sincere, and protracted hunt for it (1:7–9:18). Even after obtaining a measure of wisdom, the wise man recognizes that he still has much to learn, so he remains teachable and continues to search for wisdom (1:5; 9:9). Those who think they are wise already will see no need to embark on the quest for wisdom, and are condemned to a life of ignorance as a result (3:7; 26:12).

## Text and Translation of Proverbs

The book of Proverbs presents many difficulties in translation. Part of this is due to the lack of a larger context to understand the point being made. Part of it is due to the use rare words or grammatical constructions, and ongoing debates regarding the nature of Hebrew verb tenses. Part of it is due to basic disagreement as to the interpretation of various individual proverbs. Regardless of these difficulties, those who are not able to read and analyze the Hebrew text for themselves should choose as literal a translation as possible for reading and studying the book of Proverbs. A good translation of Proverbs will represent the original as closely as possible, thereby allowing the reader to ponder the meaning for himself. The dynamic and paraphrastic translations are terrible in Proverbs, since they read like commentaries—commentaries which are sometimes right, but which often completely misinterpret a saying. Reader beware!

## Outline of Proverbs

*Summary Outline*

I. Preface 1:1-7
II. Address to the Son 1:8–9:18
III. Proverbs of Solomon 10:1–24:34
IV. Solomonic Proverbs Added by Hezekiah's Men 25:1–29:27
V. Words of Agur and Lemuel 30:1–31:31

*Expanded Outline*

**I. Preface 1:1-7**
  A. The author 1:1

4. Concerning the weak of character 25:25-28
      a. Things refreshing and unpalatable 25:25-26
      b. On self-restraint 25:27-28
5. Concerning fools 26:1-12
6. Concerning sluggards 26:13-16
7. Concerning meddlers 26:17-19
8. Concerning injurious speakers 26:20-28
      a. On contentious speech 26:20-21
      b. On gossip 26:22
      c. On flattery 26:23-28
9. Concerning yourself 27:1-27
      a. Warning against boasting 27:1-2
      b. Things heavy and heavier 27:3-6
      c. Things fitting and unfitting 27:7-8
      d. The value of friends 27:9-10
      e. The value of prudence 27:11-12
      f. The value of discernment 27:13-14
      g. The bane of the incorrigible woman 27:15-16
      h. The value of good service 27:17-18
      i. On man's heart and eyes 27:19-20
      j. On tests of character 27:21-22
      k. Exhortation to diligence 27:23-27
  C. Mainly antithetical proverbs 28:1–29:27

**V. Words of Agur and Lemuel 30:1–31:31**
  A. The words of Agur 30:1-33
    1. Superscription 30:1a
    2. The commitment to fidelity to God and His Word 30:1b-9
      a. The mystery of God as known by general revelation 30:1b-4
      b. The trustworthiness of unmixed special revelation 30:5-6
      c. The prayer to avoid falsehood, poverty, and riches 30:7-9
    3. Admonition against slander 30:10
    4. Numerical sayings 30:11-31
      a. Four things incorrigible 30:11-14
      b. Observation on a thing insatiable 30:15a
      c. Four things insatiable 30:15b-16
      d. Observation on a thing incorrigible 30:17
      e. Four things inscrutable 30:18-19
      f. Observation on a thing inscrutable 30:20
      g. Four things intolerable 30:21-23
      h. Four things inconsiderable but intelligent 30:24-28
      i. Four things imperial 30:29-31
    5. Admonition against contention 30:32-33
  B. The words of Lemuel 31:1-31
    1. Superscription 31:1
    2. Advice to a future king 31:2-9
    3. The virtuous wife 31:10-31

## Structure and Argument of Proverbs

The overall organization of the book of Proverbs is clear, although the principles governing the order of individual proverbs and sections of instruction are much more complex. The book has five main divisions: a preface (1:1-7), an address to the son (1:8–9:18), the original collection Solomon's proverbs (10:1–24:34), Solomonic proverbs added by Hezekiah's men (25:1–29:27), and the words of Agur and Lemuel (30:1–31:31).

### *Preface, 1:1-7*

The book of Proverbs begins with a general introduction (1:1-7), which states its author, purpose, and the all-important thesis statement that sets it apart from the other so-called "wisdom literature" of the ancient world: "The fear of Yahweh is the beginning of knowledge; but the foolish despise wisdom and instruction."

### *Address to the Son 1:8–9:18*

The first major section of the body of the book of Proverbs, 1:8–9:18, consists of a long series of addresses from the father/teacher to his son/pupil. This section is generally written to a male audience, and especially young males (boyhood to late teens). It is especially appropriate for an adolescent male Bible study. Some of the divisions in this section are marked by an address to "My son," though some are marked by a shift in subject (e.g., 1:20). The "son" is an innocent, inexperienced youth whom Solomon seeks to put onto the path of life while keeping him off of the path of death. In this section, Solomon positively extols wisdom and gives general teaching about the importance of wisdom, its nature and benefits, and how to attain it, while he negatively warns against the perils of folly, especially the adulterous woman.

The body of the book begins with a warning to the son against evil associations (1:8-19), which is followed naturally by a warning concerning the ruin which follows a refusal of wisdom's call (1:20-33). Solomon then commends to the son the search for wisdom, asserting that such a search will in fact be successful, and that it will yield blessing and make one virtuous (2:1-22). In the next paragraph, 3:1-12, Solomon urges the son to obey and honor Yahweh, since the fear of Yahweh is inseparably linked with the acquiring of wisdom and consequent blessing. Solomon then extols the great benefits of wisdom, in order to motivate the son to search for it (3:13-26). This is followed by another paragraph which links moral virtue with wisdom and blessing, in an exhortation to act justly and uprightly (3:27-35).[3] Chapter 4 consists of three exhortations to sons which repeat earlier material in different language for the sake of reinforcement: an exhortation to acquire wisdom (4:1-9), an exhortation to avoid evil company (4:10-19), and an exhortation to take diligent care to follow Solomon's instruction (4:20-27). The warning to take heed to oneself is followed, appropriately, by an extended warning against the peril of the adulteress, which is the most dangerous trap for young men (5:1-23). Chapter 5 has three sections: the paradox of the "strange" woman (5:1-6), the warning against sexual sin and its consequences (5:7-14), and the admonition to marital fidelity (5:15-23). More general instruction on wise living is then given in 6:1-5 (on extrication from a mess created by foolish decisions), in 6:6-11 (a warning against sloth), in 6:12-15 (on the demise of the perverse man), and in 6:16-19 (on seven things hated by Yahweh), before returning to the warning against adultery in 6:20-35. The snare of the adulteress is then vividly illustrated in ch. 7 by a

---

[3] Strictly speaking "wisdom" and "righteousness" are two different, though interdependent, concepts: the former is an intellectual quality, while the latter is a moral quality. The same distinction exists between "folly" (an intellectual deficiency) and "wickedness" (a moral deficiency), though the two are interlinked.

textbook example of a young man falling into her trap. As the adulteress is the personification of folly, Solomon finally contrasts her in ch. 8 with the personification of wisdom.[4] This is the positive call to which the son should in fact yield (8:1-11). Wisdom commends itself (8:12-21), is eternal (8:22-31), and is the key to obtaining blessing (8:32-36). The first major section of the book concludes in ch. 9 with further personifications of wisdom and folly, and their contrasting calls. Wisdom is personified in 9:1-12, first with her feast and invitation (9:1-6), then with her teaching (9:7-12). This is followed by one further warning against the woman of folly, i.e., the adulteress (9:13-18).

### *Proverbs of Solomon, 10:1–24:34*

The second major division of the book of Proverbs is clearly marked by the heading of 10:1: "The Proverbs of Solomon." Hereafter follow short maxims, in contrast to the longer units observed in chs. 1–9. The shortest proverbs are in 10:1–22:16; other than 19:7, each verse from 10:1 to 22:16 consists of a single two-part saying. Within this section, 10:1–15:33 consist mainly of antithetical (contrastive) proverbs, with some proverbs of comparison interspersed. These proverbs generally contrast righteous and wicked lives. The remaining short sayings, 16:1–22:16, are mainly observations on life and conduct which are designed to encourage wise, righteous living.

The next subunit, 22:17–24:34, consists mainly of longer proverbs or sayings. This unit may be divided into two sections: sayings concerning various practices (22:17–23:35), and sayings concerning various people (24:1-34). The final part of this section, 24:23-34, is prefaced by its own heading: "These also are [sayings] of the wise" (24:23a). This could be read to indicate that 24:23-34 are non-Solomonic proverbs, although 24:33-34 are duplicated from 6:10-11; perhaps these are sayings which Solomon borrowed from other wise men. When the book was first written, the warning against laziness in 24:30-34 probably formed the close of the Solomonic section, with chs. 30–31 immediately following. Just as the introductory section in which Solomon gave instruction to sons was concluded by a warning against the personification of folly—the adulteress—the section of Solomon's general teaching on principles of wise living is concluded by a warning against the sluggard. Laziness is thereby singled out as an eminent characteristic of fools. Every wise men is characterized by diligence and conscientiousness, whereas fools are lazy and irresponsible.

An attempt to trace the connection of thought from one proverb to the next throughout chs. 10–24 would be a major project, as paragraphs are often only a single verse, especially in 10:1–22:16. Some general structural principles have been observed, such as the fact that proverbs which mention the name of Yahweh tend to come in clusters, or the fact that 10:18-21 contains a series of proverbs about speech. Often there will be two or three proverbs in a row which have a similar theme, but it is just as common to have seemingly unrelated proverbs juxtaposed. Clearly the overall arrangement of the proverbs is not topical, which makes the logic of their order an extremely complex question. This order must be the one Solomon made, and it must be intentional, which means there must be some overall rationale behind it, and perhaps some argument that is made in the flow of the book. One advantage of a non-topical arrangement is that Solomon is able to return to the same themes again and again, sometimes even using identical or nearly identical language to make the same point. In most instances, if there were ten proverbs in a row that were all on the same subject, it would be easy for the reader simply to read the paragraph and forget it, or to lose interest by the end of the section. But by scattering related proverbs throughout the book, the reader is reminded of these principles again and again as he reads. If he is not sufficiently prompted to consider the matter by the first proverb, he may be by the second or third on the same subject. There are also subtle connections in the organization, as one proverb somehow places the

---

[4] Wisdom is personified as a woman, partly because the Hebrew word for "wisdom" is a feminine noun, and partly to form a contrast with the adulteress. Solomon certainly is not claiming that women are wiser than men, as some say, since folly is also personified as a woman.

reader in the right frame of mind to listen to the next and the next. Only so great a sage as Solomon, under the Holy Spirit's direction, could have crafted such an arrangement. A dissertation is needed to give a more detailed explanation of Solomon's arrangement, and to trace this through the book.

It is typical for pastors and Bible teachers to teach the proverbs by topic. This method is contrary to the wisdom of Solomon's original arrangement, and seems to assume that the inspired arrangement is disorganized or random. The true way to teach the proverbs is in the order Solomon put them, going verse by verse through the book. It is not just the words of the book that are inspired and instructive, but the arrangement as well. Those who teach verses in isolation from the context of the book, and without any attempt to find and communicate a synthetic argument, are not actually teaching the biblical text. Another problem endemic to topical teaching is that much of the book is normally skipped, or at least isolated proverbs here and there, with the result that some of God's counsel is ignored.

### *Solomonic Proverbs Added by Hezekiah's Men, 25:1–29:27*

Chapters 25–29 are Solomonic proverbs, but ones added to the book during the time of Hezekiah. These proverbs consist mainly of longer sayings which are linked together according to a complex pattern, often following a concatenated structure. Once again, a more thorough study is needed to answer the crucial question of the logic of this complex arrangement, and to trace the flow of thought from one verse to the next, and from one section to the next; understanding these connections is important to understanding the individual sayings themselves. Chapters 25–27 consist mainly of longer sayings or thematically arranged proverbs which are generally comparative rather than antithetical. The sayings in chs. 25–27 also have as a common thread that they are all about persons. The first two groups of people spoken of, kings (25:2-7) and neighbors (25:8-20), could be good or bad. The next six groups of sayings are about morally corrupt persons: adversaries (25:21-24), the weak of character (25:25-28), fools (26:1-12), sluggards (26:13-16), meddlers (26:17-19), and injurious speakers (26:20-28). The final person spoken of/to is simply oneself (27:1-27). Each of these groups of sayings also contains smaller thematic subgroups. Chapters 28–29 consist mainly of antithetical (contrastive) one-line proverbs which are generally not arranged in larger units.

### *Words of Agur and Lemuel, 30:1–31:31*

Chapters 30–31 form a special capstone which is designed to bring the book of Proverbs to a fitting conclusion; these chapters are not merely tacked onto the end of the book as an appendix, as some claim. Chapter 30, consisting of the words of Agur, is one of the Bible's great chapters, a wellspring of deep wisdom; it demands careful contemplation. After the heading (30:1a), the Agur's speech opens with a statement of his commitment to fidelity to God and His Word (30:1b-9). This is followed by an admonition against slander (30:10), a series of numerical sayings interspersed with observations on the things these sayings describe (30:11-31), and a closing admonition against contention (30:32-33).

Chapter 31 is called "the words of Lemuel," but really originates with his mother, who made him memorize these words. After the superscription (31:1) follows a section of advice to a future king (31:2-9). The book of Proverbs concludes with the description of the worthy woman, using an alphabetic acrostic as an aid to memory (31:10-31). This oracle was given to a man, not a woman, and it is primarily intended as advice for unmarried men: men are to seek to marry a woman like this. In the opening chapters of the book, large sections were devoted to warning young men against the adulteress. It is fitting that the book should conclude positively, by informing young men about the ideal woman. Perowne comments:

> The picture here drawn of woman in her proper sphere of home, as a wife and a mother and the
> mistress of a household, stands out in bright relief against the dark sketches of woman degraded

by impurity, or marred by imperfections, which are to be found in earlier chapters of this Book (ii. 16-20; v. 1-23; vii.; xxii. 14; xxiii. 27, 28, and xi. 22; xix. 13; xxi. 19). Corruptio optimi pessima. ["The corruption of the best is the worst."] We have here woman occupying and adorning her rightful place. . . . It is an expansion of the earlier proverb: "Whoso findeth a wife findeth a good *thing*, and obtaineth favour of the Lord" (xviii. 22).[5]

Unlike the woman of folly, who is always out and about (7:11-12), the virtuous woman (or "wife") remains at home and attends to the needs of her household. The virtuous woman brings blessing and honor to her husband (31:11-12, 23, 28-29), while the woman of folly cheats on him (7:19-20). The virtuous woman serves her husband and her household, whereas the woman of folly only serves herself. The virtuous woman builds, while the woman of folly destroys. The virtuous woman is, finally, a woman who fears Yahweh, and who therefore is wise (31:30; cf. 1:7). The description of the virtuous wife thus brings to a fitting conclusion to the argument which was begun in the opening chapters of the book.

---

[5] Perowne, *Proverbs*, 188.

## Bibliography for Proverbs

Generally speaking, a good commentary on the book of Proverbs will be a commentary which attempts to find order and structure throughout the book. A poor commentary is one that sees the inspired structure as random and disorganized, and rearranges the book by topic.

Aitken, Kenneth T. *Proverbs*. The Daily Study Bible. Philadelphia: Westminster Press, 1986.

Arnot, William. *Laws from Heaven for Life on Earth: Illustrations of the Book of Proverbs*. London: T. Nelson and Sons, 1863.

Atkinson, David. *The Message of Proverbs: Wisdom for Life*. The Bible Speaks Today. Downers Grove, IL: Inter-Varsity Press, 1996.

Bridges, Charles. *An Exposition of the Book of Proverbs*. New York: Robert Carter, 1850.

Buzzell, Sid S. "Proverbs." Pages 901-74 in *The Bible Knowledge Commentary: Old Testament*, ed. John F. Walvoord and Roy B. Zuck. Colorado Springs: Chariot Victor, 1985.

Delitzsch, Franz. *Biblical Commentary on the Proverbs of Solomon*. M. G. Easton, trans. 2 vols. Reprint: Grand Rapids: Eerdmans, 1950.

Ironside, H. A. *Notes on the Book of Proverbs*. Neptune, NJ: Loizeaux Brothers, 1908.

Jensen, Irving L. *Proverbs*. Chicago: Moody Press, 1982.

Kidner, Derek. *The Proverbs: An Introduction and Commentary*. Tyndale Old Testament Commentaries, ed. D. J. Wiseman, vol. 15. Downers Grove, IL: Inter-Varsity Press, 1964.

Kitchen, John A. *Proverbs*. Mentor. Ross-shire, Great Britain: Christian Focus, 2006.
    **Note:** Kitchen seems to be quite good.

Longman, Tremper, III. *Proverbs*. Baker Commentary on the Old Testament Wisdom and Psalms. Grand Rapids: Baker, 2006.

MacDonald, William. *Enjoying the Proverbs*. Rev. ed. Kansas City, KS: Walterick Publishers, 1982.
    **Note:** The first edition was called *Listen, My Son*.

McGee, J. Vernon. "Proverbs." In *Thru the Bible with J. Vernon McGee*, vol. 3, 1-104. Nashville: Thomas Nelson, 1982.

Miller, John W. *Proverbs*. Believers Church Bible Commentary. Scottdale, PA: Herald Press, 2004.

Murphy, Roland E. *Proverbs*. Word Biblical Commentary, vol. 22. Nashville: Thomas Nelson, 1998.
    **Note:** Murphy's translation is not especially good, but it can be helpful. His textual notes and bibliographic information are also helpful. His interpretation is less helpful, since he was a Roman Catholic. Perhaps worth looking at.

Perowne, T. T. *The Proverbs: With Introduction and Notes*. Cambridge Bible for Schools and Colleges. Cambridge: Cambridge, 1899.

Plumptre, E. H. "Proverbs." In *The Holy Bible with an Explanatory and Critical Commentary*, ed. F. C. Cook, vol. 4, 513-618. Cambridge: C. J. Clay, 1892.

Ross, Allen P. "Proverbs." Pages 881-1134 in *The Expositor's Bible Commentary*, vol. 5. Grand Rapids: Zondervan, 1991.

———. "Proverbs." Pages 21-252 in *The Expositor's Bible Commentary: Revised Edition*, vol. 6. Grand Rapids: Zondervan, 2008.

Scott, R. B. Y. *Proverbs; Ecclesiastes: Introduction, Translation, and Notes.* 2nd ed. Anchor Bible, vol. 18. Garden City, NY: Doubleday, 1974.

Steveson, Peter A. *A Commentary on Proverbs.* Greenville, SC: BJU Press, 2001.
    **Note:** Steveson was a professor at Bob Jones University, and so is theologically conservative. Unfortunately, he thinks the proverbs are ordered randomly.

Toy, Crawford H. *A Critical and Exegetical Commentary on the Book of Proverbs.* International Critical Commentary. Edinburgh: T. & T. Clark, 1899.

Waltke, Bruce K. *The Book of Proverbs: Chapters 1–15.* New International Commentary on the Old Testament. Grand Rapids: Eerdmans, 2004.

Waltke, Bruce K. *The Book of Proverbs: Chapters 15–31.* New International Commentary on the Old Testament. Grand Rapids: Eerdmans, 2005.

Wardlaw, Ralph. *Lectures on the Book of Proverbs.* J. S. Wardlaw, ed. 2 vols. London: A. Fullerton, 1861.

Wright, J. Robert, and Thomas C. Oden, eds. *Proverbs, Ecclesiastes, Song of Solomon.* Ancient Christian Commentary on Scripture: Old Testament, vol. 9. Downers Grove, IL: InterVarsity Press, 2005.

# Interpretive Guide to Ecclesiastes

The book of Ecclesiastes is an investigation of human life, of the human experience in this world. This is the subject of the entire book, to which various themes are added as Solomon develops his account of the investigation. Ecclesiastes is the most philosophical book in the Bible by far, the end-all philosophy treatise, designed to be appreciated by deep thinkers. It is a book that cannot be read casually; each verse contains wise and often enigmatic statements that require deep thinking to understand and appreciate. The superficial explanation of the book is to write it off as a statement of the philosophy of the unbeliever. Those who view Ecclesiastes as an unbeliever's philosophy do not understand the wisdom of this book, nor do they have a proper outlook on life.

Ecclesiastes is a gritty, honest, plain book about life. Nothing is glossed over or sugarcoated or avoided, and there is no silver bullet offered to eliminate human suffering. The reason? It is only by maintaining a realistic perspective that one can deal effectively with the troubles and problems of life. The laughter of fools is only an anesthetic, a kind of happiness that will not sustain a person through life's toughest ordeals. Fools live at a superficial level, in order to avoid thinking about the tough things in life and the reality of death.

Ecclesiastes is not intended to make people who read it depressed. It is rather intended to demonstrate to people who understand how difficult life is that they can actually bear life's miseries and live with a measure of happiness.

## Author

The author of the book is called קֹהֶלֶת (*Qoheleth*), "the preacher," referring to Solomon's position as an instructor of his people.

> Although the name of Solomon is not prefixed to this book as it is to the Proverbs and the Song of Songs, yet the description of the author (i. 1, and i. 12) applies so definitely to him and to no other, that it answers the same purpose as if he were named. Accordingly this book is placed, in the most ancient Jewish and Christian lists, between the other two books attributed to him, and the constant tradition of the Jewish and Christian Churches has handed down Solomon without question as the author.[1]

The author of this book clearly views himself as presenting the definitive study of human life, which implies that his wisdom was unparalleled. He also says that he "increased more than all that were before me in Jerusalem" (2:9), which is something that only Solomon could have said. The identification of the author as "the son of David, king in Jerusalem" (1:1) also identifies him as Solomon. Additional evidence for Solomonic authorship of both Ecclesiastes and the Song of Songs is that both books use the relative particle שֶׁ much more frequently than anywhere else in the OT, showing that both were written by the same man. Linguistic arguments against Solomonic authorship of Ecclesiastes lack proof, and are merely an excuse used by unbelieving scholars to reject the clear affirmation of the text.

Ecclesiastes is a book of reflections, as the wisest man who ever lived looked back on his rich and varied life experiences and recounts his lifelong effort to find the key to explaining reality. Much of this book sounds as if it was written by a man who has suffered much in life. It sounds like the author has drunk deeply from the cup of life's injustices, and has been in constant distress and agony. The ironic

---

[1] W. T. Bullock, "Ecclesiastes" (in *The Holy Bible with an Explanatory and Critical Commentary*, ed. F. C. Cook, vol. 4; Cambridge: C. J. Clay, 1892), 619.

reality is that Solomon had one of the softest, most peaceful, most pleasurable lives of anybody in human history, at least from the perspective of an external observer. However, he carefully pondered all that he saw, and developed deep reflections on what life was really like—and therefore he fully recognizes the plight of those who are less fortunate. Throughout the book life is presented accurately, and injustice is neither glossed over nor explained away—Solomon just says, "That's the way life is." There is no more accurate or objective portrayal of life than the one we find in this book of Ecclesiastes.

## Date and Occasion of Writing

It is clear that the author of Ecclesiastes is an old man who is giving his final reflections on his long investigation of human life (see especially 2:1-11; 7:28; 12:1-7). Since Solomon died in 930 B.C., Ecclesiastes may have been composed in or around the year 931. The occasion of writing was Solomon's approaching death, before which he left to the people the account of his total investigation of human life.

## Purpose and Message

The purpose of Ecclesiastes is to investigate human life. The message of Ecclesiastes is, everything in this life is futile and temporary, because life itself does not last; but in spite of the vanity of life, God has given a wonderful gift to men: we can enjoy the moment, enjoy the mundane, and take pleasure in ordinary work. It is good for man to enjoy God's gift of life, to value wisdom, and to walk in the fear of God.

## Outline of Ecclesiastes

I. The Introductory Affirmation 1:1-11
    A. Heading 1:1
    B. The vanity of life observed 1:2-11
II. Solomon's Search for Meaning in Life and Its Failure 1:12–2:23
    A. Solomon's unique position to see life, and his failure to find meaning in it 1:12-18
    B. The search for meaning in worldly comforts and its failure 2:1-11
    C. The search for meaning in wisdom and its failure 2:12-17
    D. The vanity of labor 2:18-23
    E. The value of labor 2:24-26
III. God's Sovereign Design in the Human Experience 3:1-22
    A. God's design for enjoyment in the midst of human futility and ignorance 3:1-15
    B. God's design for life's outcome, and the proper response 3:16-22
IV. Exhortation to Enjoy the Here and Now 4:1–5:20
    A. The grief of labor 4:1-16
        1. The greatness of life's suffering 4:1-3
        2. The grief of labor and laziness 4:4-6
        3. The grief of laboring alone 4:7-12
        4. The grief of ruling poorly and well 4:13-16
    B. The dangers of labor 5:1-17
        1. The danger of thoughtless religious service 5:1-7
        2. The danger of official injustice 5:8-9
        3. The danger of loving money 5:10-12
        4. The danger of hoarding riches 5:13-17
    C. Conclusion 5:18-20

V. The Inscrutability of Life 6:1–8:15
   A. The vanity of the workaholic's life 6:1-6
   B. The vanity of life's endless cycle 6:7-9
   C. Man's ignorance 6:10-12
   D. The value of sobriety 7:1-4
   E. The vanity of the fool's path to pleasure 7:5-7
   F. The patience of wisdom 7:8-10
   G. The value and instruction of wisdom 7:11-14
   H. Apparent inconsistencies in God's treatment of men 7:15-18
   I. Wise observations on life 7:19-22
   J. The partial discovery of the key to explaining the human experience: gender differences 7:23-29
   K. Obedience to authorities as the wise response to life's uncertainties 8:1-8
   L. Reflections on apparent inconsistencies in God's dealings with man 8:9-15
VI. Summary of the Search for the Ultimate Explanation of the Human Experience 8:16–9:10
   A. The impossibility of finding the explanation 8:16–9:1
   B. The ultimate cause of futility in life 9:2-6
   C. Wise living in light of life's futility 9:7-10
VII. Instruction Based on Solomon's Investigation of Life 9:11–12:8
   A. Observations on the uncertainty of life 9:11-12
   B. Observations on wisdom 9:13-16
   C. Observations on folly 9:17–10:4
   D. Observations on incongruities 10:5-7
   E. Observations on misfortune 10:8-11
   F. Observation on wise and foolish speech 10:12-15
   G. Observation on wise and foolish governance 10:16-20
   H. Instruction on the use of resources 11:1-6
   I. Instruction on the use of life 11:7-8
   J. Instruction on the use of youth 11:9–12:8
VIII. Epilogue 12:9-14
   A. The career of the Preacher 12:9-10
   B. Observation on the words of wisdom 12:11
   C. Admonition against being overly studious 12:12
   D. Conclusion: the ultimate principle by which to live 12:13-14

**Argument of Ecclesiastes**

Ecclesiastes begins with the discouraging observation that life is vain because it does not endure and is not remembered, and the book continues with this theme throughout. But there is another, brighter theme running alongside it, which is this: human existence on earth is precious, and ought to be valued and maximized, rather than wasted. Because life is so short, and the explanation for reality cannot be discovered, the best thing man can do is recognize that life is a gift from God, and that it should be enjoyed. This means enjoying all the good things in the world that God has given man to make life pleasant (9:7-9). It means enjoying the good times (11:8) and dwelling on the present during the days of your youth (11:9–12:1). It means doing all of your work with your full effort and best ability, because you will not have another chance to do it (9:10). Since nothing in this life endures, it is best to enjoy each moment as well as one can. However, life is also full of pain and injustice, no matter what one's situation, and if one is in a good position today, he cannot know whether he will still be in that position tomorrow.

It should be noted that most or all of the futility Solomon complains about is a direct result of the fall, and is not part of life as God originally created it and intended for it to be. The ultimate futility that

Solomon keeps returning to is death, which makes no distinction between men, and which ends all the accomplishments of one's life. Other futilities Solomon complains of are related to folly and to the injustices of life, both of which result from the fall. Life has become futile because of the fall. Death makes life futile because nothing that man can do will endure, and man himself does not endure. However, while we have meaninglessness in this life, it is not ultimate meaninglessness; only unbelieving men have ultimate meaninglessness.

### *The Introductory Affirmation, 1:1-11*

The first main paragraph gives the theme of the work, which is the total futility of life.[2] Solomon observes that life is vaporous, or futile, because nothing lasts—nothing that is good in life lasts, nothing that is bad lasts, youth does not last, money does not last, and wisdom does not last, because life itself does not last.

### *Solomon's Search for Meaning in Life and Its Failure, 1:12–2:26*

In 1:12–2:23, Solomon describes how he undertook a great search for meaning in life, and how this search failed to find meaning. As king of Israel and a man of unparalleled wisdom, Solomon was in a unique position to understand life, yet he discovered that wisdom and folly are both ultimately a striving after wind (1:12-18). Solomon next searched for meaning in the physical comforts of this world, amassing a fortune without equal, and creating great works—only to find that there was no true profit in all of his labor (2:1-11). Solomon then turned once again to consider wisdom, and while he found that wisdom is a wonderful thing, he realized that it ultimately does not remove the vanity of life, since the wise man will die just as the fool (2:12-16). When Solomon reflected on the bitter reality of death in a sin-cursed world, this man who had everything sank into depression (2:17). He realized that the great works he had made would not endure, and may be left to unworthy posterity (2:18-23). However, though Solomon recognized the vanity of labor, he also discovered the value of labor (2:24-26): God has given men the ability to take pleasure in ordinary work, even though it does not last. Thus the solution to life's vanity is not to wallow in depression, but to stay busy working, eating, and enjoying the things of life, since this is what makes human existence bearable—and, actually, enjoyable and fulfilling.

### *God's Sovereign Design in the Human Experience, 3:1-22*

Solomon follows the account of his failed search for something lasting in life with an account of God's sovereign design in the human experience (3:1-22). He notes in 3:1-8 fourteen pairs of activities for which God has appointed a proper time in life. In each pair, the one activity undoes the work of the other, leading to the conclusion in 3:9-10 is that there is no ultimate profit in labor because man's work does not last. However, God has designed man to enjoy life, in spite of the objective fact of human futility and ignorance (3:11-15). God has determined, in His sovereignty, to allow injustice to exist in life, and to

---

[2] The Hebrew word הֶבֶל means "meaningless" in the sense of "vaporous," not "purposeless." Solomon is not arguing that life is pointless or purposeless, but that it is vaporous. Possible translations of הֶבֶל include "uselessness," "vaporous," "fleeting," "transitory," "futility," "vanity," "emptiness." Some translations have "meaningless," but the validity of this rendering is debatable. When Solomon says that something is הֶבֶל, what he means is that it does not last.

wait until a later time to bring final judgment upon the wicked and the righteous, since all die; therefore, there is nothing better for a person to do than to take joy in his life and in his work (3:16-22).

### *Exhortation to Enjoy the Here and Now, 4:1–5:20*

In 4:1–5:20, Solomon commends enjoyment of the here and now as the only anesthetic to life's futility and suffering, in spite of the futility of labor. He begins in 4:1-3 by simply observing the astounding severity of the sufferings of life. He then observes how both labor and laziness are grief-bringing activities (4:4-6). He observes in 4:7-12 how laboring alone is grievous and futile. The next grievous labor he considers is that of governing, since a reign which begins well seldom ends well (4:13-16). Solomon then observes the danger of going overboard in religious labor by making foolish vows or approaching God too frequently, and therefore thoughtlessly and carelessly (5:1-7). He observes how even the governing officials frequently oppress poor laborers, although the king himself eats the produce of the land (5:8-9). Solomon warns against the love of money (5:10-12), since the one who loves money can never have enough to be content with it, and his money actually brings him grief, not happiness. Solomon likewise warns against hoarding riches, since they cannot be kept after one dies, and therefore have no real and lasting profit (5:13-17). However, in spite of all of the griefs and dangers of labor, Solomon repeats his conclusion that the ability to rejoice in labor and to enjoy the good things of life is a gift from God, and that it should be received and used in order to stay occupied and not to think much about the grief and futility of life (5:18-20).

### *The Inscrutability of Life, 6:1–8:15*

In ch. 6, Solomon begins to move into a discussion of the inscrutability of life—a subject which he already introduced in 3:11. He begins by making observations about the way life works, hoping that by so doing he might work his way to a grand solution to life's riddle. He observes the man who is, whether by choice or compulsion, a workaholic, and does not have time to enjoy life (6:1-2). His conclusion: the workaholic's life is wasted; he would have been better off taking an easier path to the grave, since that is where all men end up (6:3-6). Life is an endless cycle of appetite and labor to fulfill the appetite, but it is all in vain because it fails to last (6:7-9). Further, man cannot adequately prepare for what lies ahead in life, because he does not know what it will be (6:10-12).

Solomon next observes that sorrow is better than laughter because the end of all men is death, and shallow mirth cannot deal with the real issues of life (7:1-4). The fool's path to pleasure is short-lived and leads to long term pain (7:5-7). The wise man has the patience to persevere to the conclusion of a matter (7:8), to suppress his anger (7:9), and to recognize the benefit of living in the present (7:10). Wisdom is invaluable as a tool to understand life; and even though man cannot understand the specific reason why things happen the way they do, wisdom leads a man to realize that God does not want him to take anything in life for granted (7:11-14). For this reason, there are apparent inconsistencies in God's treatment of the righteous and the wicked; however, in spite of these inconsistencies it is still good to fear God (7:15-18). Solomon then reflects again on the value of wisdom (7:19-22).

In 7:23-29, Solomon summarizes the results of his efforts to understand ultimate ends and causes in life, and admits that while wisdom ultimately eludes even the wise, he has found a partial key to explaining the human experience in the differences between men and women.

In view of the wise man's inability to find the ultimate account of life, Solomon counsels his hearers to obey and respect the authorities as the best way to prepare for life's uncertain and uncontrollable happenings (8:1-8). However, there are in fact apparent inconsistencies in God's dealings with man, for which Solomon has no specific explanation, but still affirms that it is better to fear God and to enjoy life (8:9-15).

*Summary of the Search for the Ultimate*
*Explanation of the Human Experience, 8:16–9:10*

In 8:16–9:10, Solomon summarizes the results of his search for the ultimate explanation of the human experience. He concludes that it is absolutely impossible for man to discover the explanation of all reality in the world, though some such explanation must exist; God has simply placed a veil over tomorrow (8:16–9:1). Man's life is ultimately futile because it comes to an end (9:2-6). The wise response to life's futility is to enjoy life and live it to the full, maximizing one's God-given potential (9:7-10). We ought not to give up on life, but rather should pursue and maximize it, should live in the present, and should enjoy life while it lasts.

*Instruction Based on Solomon's Investigation of Life, 9:11–12:8*

In 9:11–12:8, Solomon offers instruction on wise living, as a reflection on his search for the ultimate account of the human experience. First, in 9:11-12, he observes how life is uncertain, and possession of superior ability does not guarantee success. Wisdom is extremely profitable for success in life, and yet does not guarantee worldly prosperity (9:13-16). Folly, on the other hand, destroys much good and also destroys the fool (9:17–10:4). Life has many incongruities and improprieties, which Solomon observes in 10:5-7. Solomon next observes how a man's work, whatever it may be, eventually will end up destroying him through misfortune (10:8-11). He observes wise and foolish speech in 10:12-15, and wise and foolish leadership in 10:16-20.

After the observations in 9:11–10:20, Solomon finally gives instruction in ch. 11 on the use of human endowments. In 11:1-6, Solomon counsels his hearers to distribute their monetary resources broadly, in order to have blessing return to them in the end, regardless of life's calamities. Life is a blessing, not a curse; it is good to experience life, and the more the better, while maintaining a realistic perspective (11:7-8). Youth in particular is a blessing, and should be used to revel in the newness of things and in the full use of one's natural faculties, before all is lost in old age and death, which ends life and therefore makes it futile (11:9–12:8).

*Epilogue, 12:9-14*

After a restatement of the conclusion in 12:8, the book of Ecclesiastes ends with an epilogue (12:9-14). The Preacher's activities as a teacher of the people are summarized in 12:9-10, with an emphasis on the great care which Solomon took to carefully craft his sayings and to give diligence to find truth. This is followed by an observation on the words of wisdom, the point of which is that there is no such thing as secular wisdom—true wisdom comes only from God, and is known only by the redeemed (12:11). However, those who love wisdom can easily fall into the trap of being overly studious and wearing themselves out while failing to enjoy life (12:12). One cannot learn or read everything, and need not and should not try; it is wise to focus on God's words rather than man's, to work smart, and to take breaks. The book of Ecclesiastes concludes with a statement of the ultimate principle by which man ought to live: fear God and keep His commandments (12:13). Our future in this life may not be certain, but we all know exactly what is coming afterward, and we ought to live in preparation for it (12:14).

## Bibliography for Ecclesiastes

Bartholomew, Craig G. *Ecclesiastes*. Baker Commentary on the Old Testament Wisdom and Psalms, ed. Tremper Longman III. Grand Rapids: Baker, 2009.

Barton, George Aaron. *A Critical and Exegetical Commentary on the Book of Ecclesiastes*. International Critical Commentary. Edinburgh: T. & T. Clark, 1908.

Bullock, W. T. "Ecclesiastes." In *The Holy Bible with an Explanatory and Critical Commentary*, ed. F. C. Cook, vol. 4, 619-63. Cambridge: C. J. Clay, 1892.

Compton, Charles. "The Argument of Ecclesiastes." Unpublished Th.M. thesis. Dallas Theological Seminary, 1974.

Crenshaw, James L. *Ecclesiastes: A Commentary*. Old Testament Library. Philadelphia: Westminster, 1987.

De Haan, Richard W., and Herbert Vander Lugt. *The Art of Staying off Dead-End Streets*. Wheaton, IL: Victor Books, 1974.

Delitzsch, Franz. *Commentary on the Song of Songs and Ecclesiastes*. Translated by M. G. Easton. Biblical Commentary on the Old Testament. Reprint: Grand Rapids: Eerdmans, 1950.

Eaton, Michael A. *Ecclesiastes: An Introduction and Commentary*. Tyndale Old Testament Commentaries. Downers Grove, IL: Inter-Varsity Press, 1983.

Fredericks, Daniel C. and Daniel J. Estes. *Ecclesiastes & the Song of Songs*. Apollos Old Testament Commentary, ed. David W. Baker and Gordon J. Wenham, vol. 16. Downers Grove, IL: InterVarsity Press, 2010.

Glenn, Donald R. "Ecclesiastes." Pages 975-1007 in *The Bible Knowledge Commentary: Old Testament*, ed. John F. Walvoord and Roy B. Zuck. Colorado Springs: Chariot Victor, 1985.

Gordis, Robert. *Koheleth—The Man and His World: A Study of Ecclesiastes*. 3rd ed. New York: Schocken Books, 1968.

Hengstenberg, E. W. *Commentary on Ecclesiastes, with Other Treatises*. Trans. D. W. Simon. Philadelphia: Smith, English, & Co., 1860.
**Note:** Hengstenberg was a great scholar, and very conservative.

Hubbard, David A. *Ecclesiastes, Song of Solomon*. Communicator's Commentary, ed. Lloyd J. Ogilvie, vol. 15B. Dallas: Word, 1991.

Kidner, Derek. *A Time to Mourn, and a Time to Dance: The Message of Ecclesiastes*. The Bible Speaks Today, ed. J. A. Moyer. Leicester, England: Inter-Varsity Press, 1976.

Krüger, Thomas. *Qoheleth: A Commentary*. Translated by O. C. Dean Jr. Edited by Klaus Baltzer. Hermeneia. Minneapolis: Fortress Press, 2004.

Leupold, H. C. *Exposition of Ecclesiastes*. Grand Rapids: Baker, 1952.

Lohfink, Norbert. *Qoheleth*. Translated by Sean McEvenue. Continental Commentaries. Minneapolis: Fortress Press, 2003.

Longman, Tremper, III. *The Book of Ecclesiastes*. New International Commentary on the Old Testament. Grand Rapids: Eerdmans, 1998.

McGee, J. Vernon. "Ecclesiastes." In *Thru the Bible with J. Vernon McGee*, vol. 3, 105-41. Nashville: Thomas Nelson, 1982.

Murphy, Roland E. *Ecclesiastes*. Word Biblical Commentary, vol. 23A. Nashville: Thomas Nelson, 1992.

Plumptre, E. H. *Ecclesiastes*. The Cambridge Bible for Schools and Colleges. Cambridge: Cambridge, 1888.

Provan, Iain. *Ecclesiastes, Song of Songs*. NIV Application Commentary. Grand Rapids: Zondervan, 2001.

Scott, R. B. Y. *Proverbs; Ecclesiastes: Introduction, Translation, and Notes*. 2nd ed. Anchor Bible, vol. 18. Garden City, NY: Doubleday, 1974.

Seow, Choon-Leong. *Ecclesiastes: A New Translation with Introduction and Commentary*. Anchor Bible, vol. 18C. New York: Doubleday, 1997.

Shepherd, Jerry E. "Ecclesiastes." Pages 253-365 in *The Expositor's Bible Commentary: Revised Edition*, vol. 6. Grand Rapids: Zondervan, 2008.

Wardlaw, Ralph. *Exposition of Ecclesiastes*. Philadelphia: William S. Rentoul, 1868.

Whybray, R. N. *Ecclesiastes*. New Century Bible Commentary. Grand Rapids: Eerdmans, 1989.

Wright, J. Robert, and Thomas C. Oden, eds. *Proverbs, Ecclesiastes, Song of Solomon*. Ancient Christian Commentary on Scripture: Old Testament, vol. 9. Downers Grove, IL: InterVarsity Press, 2005.

Wright, J. Stafford. "Ecclesiastes." Pages 1135-97 in *The Expositor's Bible Commentary*, vol. 5. Grand Rapids: Zondervan, 1991.

Young, Loyal. *A Commentary on the Book of Ecclesiastes*. Philadelphia: Presbyterian Board of Publication, 1865.
    **Note:** This commentary is very worth consulting, especially for Young's presentation of the argument of the book.

# Interpretive Guide to Song of Songs

The twenty-second book of the English Bible is known by two common titles, "The Song of Songs" and "The Song of Solomon." Both titles could claim support from the heading of the book, "The Song of songs, which is Solomon's" (1:1). However, Solomon composed 1,005 songs (1 Kgs 4:32), of which this was only one. Hence, this is not *the* song of Solomon's, nor is it said to be so in 1:1. This is, however, *the* song of songs—a superlative construction which refers to the best of all songs (compare the parallel expressions "God of gods," "King of kings," etc.).

No translation can preserve the striking beauty of this book's language in the original Hebrew; it is absolutely breathtaking. The choice of words used, the sentence structure, the idioms, and the phrasing are unsurpassed, even incredible. There is no song like this anywhere else in the Bible. Probably the dialogue was originally spoken, and was afterward set to music by Solomon. The original tune for this song, like the original tunes of the Psalms, has unfortunately been lost over time, although it is possible that portions of the melody have been preserved in Jewish synagogue liturgy over the millennia. But though we can no longer hear the original words sung to the original tune, as Solomon and the Shulammite sang it, many a newlywed couple could sing or recite the words with just the same passion as the original two lovers in the song. Such is the beauty of marriage—it is a gift to be exclusively enjoyed by two, and yet it may be had by all.

There is only one direct mention of God (Yah) in the Song of Songs, in an idiom in 8:6. But, as in the book of Esther, God is always assumed in the background. It is God who originally brought man and woman together in marital union, and it is God who continues to join men and women together in marriage. In the song, God is giving Solomon and his wife their passionate love for each other, and is joining them together in an unbreakable bond.

Many theologians historically, and still today, hold that there must be a deeper meaning to this book. Churchmen allegorized it as a description of the love of Christ for His church; rabbis spiritualized it as an allegory of Yahweh's love for Israel. Some theologians simply cannot fathom why an entire book of the Bible would be devoted to expressing the ideal of marital love, and why it would be called the greatest of all songs. Where is the spiritual meaning? The answer—marriage is spiritual, and marital love is the deepest and most intimate and most beautiful expression of love in human relationships. The two greatest commandments are both commands to love, and God Himself is love (Mark 12:28-31; 1 John 4:8, 16). A song which gives the truest expression of the best kind of human love, as God mysteriously joins a man and his wife in sacred union, may rightly be called the greatest of all songs; no allegorical or typological meaning need be read into it to elevate it to a higher plane. A song which celebrates and glorifies the divine institution of marriage has its rightful place in the canon of sacred writ.

This book exists in the canon of Scripture because of the great value God places on marital love. It presents an idyllic vision of marriage as the beautiful union that God created it to be—a vision which has been almost completely lost in modern society. Because of sinful man's misunderstanding and perversion of marital love, many figures in church history have been embarrassed by the Song of Songs, feeling that its portrayal of marriage is too intimate to be appropriate for public consumption. Certainly there are some things throughout the Bible that might be hard to explain to young children, or that would need to be handled delicately before a mixed audience. But there is a huge, qualitative difference between the portrayal of romantic love in the OT and its portrayal in extrabiblical ancient Near Eastern literature or the romance literature of our own time. Discussions of romantic love in extrabiblical literature are basically verbal pornography, and are written with the intent to arouse and gratify illicit sexual desires. The Song of Songs, by contrast, paints such a beautiful picture of marriage that it makes the world's cheap substitutes look pathetic by comparison. This is not a book that stirs up passions of sinful lust, but a book that leads the reader to wonder at the divine beauty of the marriage union. The Song moves people to purity, not immorality, since immorality ruins the beautiful picture of love it presents and fails to unite lovers in the pure, unbreakable bond of marriage exemplified by Solomon and the Shulammite.

## Author

The heading of this book identifies it as Solomon's song (1:1), even though Solomon, the Shulammite ("the Solomoness"—6:13), and the daughters of Jerusalem are all speakers. Solomon actually wrote the words that the three speakers uttered. Solomon is named six times in the song, and there are frequent references to his kingship and royal status. In spite of Solomon's polygamous practice, he was the ideal author of this book as David's son and heir, as the most prosperous of Israel's kings, and as the wisest man who ever lived.

There is ample internal evidence for Solomonic authorship, if only unbelieving scholars could see it. The language of this song is so high, and its celebration of marital love so perfect, that only the wisest man who ever lived could have penned its words. As a love song, this book is also far different from pagan and later Jewish poems and myths in that it is strictly a celebration of marital love, and does not cross the line into lewdness or celebrate sexual immorality. There is not so much as a hint of immoral sexual gratification in the whole song. It was obviously a servant of the one holy God who wrote it.

Critical scholars have objected to Solomonic authorship of Ecclesiastes and Song of Songs on the basis of supposedly late language. The language of these books is indeed unique, due to Solomon's unique intellectual gifting, but it is not demonstrably late. Some scholars suggest that Song of Songs was written in a northern dialect, due to the frequent use of the prefixed relative particle שֶׁ. However, while the Shulammite was likely from the north, these scholars are assuming more than they know about the characteristics of local dialects in ancient Israel and its environs over time. Solomon also uses שֶׁ frequently in Ecclesiastes, probably because he simply preferred the shortened relative as a more elevated literary style. Incidentally, the similarity in writing style between Ecclesiastes and Song of Songs is evidence that the same man penned both books. In addition, the mention of Tirzah in parallel with Jerusalem in Song 6:4 points to a date of composition during the united monarchy, since Tirzah subsequently became the capital of the northern kingdom and a rival to Jerusalem.

## Date and Occasion of Writing

This book was apparently composed and sung after the wedding ceremony and the consummation of Solomon's marriage to the Shulammite, during or shortly after their "honeymoon." Solomon reigned from 970 to 930 BC, and one would assume that this marriage took place fairly early in his reign. The Song indicates in 6:8 that Solomon had by this point in his life married sixty wives (queens) and eighty concubines (wives of secondary status), which is fourteen percent of his final number of wives and concubines (cf. 1 Kgs 11:3). It is also apparent that the Song was composed after Solomon had been given unparalleled wisdom by God, and after he had become extremely prosperous and well established as king. Without any more exact markers of a date of composition, I would suggest that the Song was written sometime in the first five to twelve years of Solomon's reign.

## Purpose and Message

The purpose of the Song of Songs is to celebrate marriage, and to illustrate how perfectly united a husband and wife become when they are married. The message of the Song of Songs is, marriage unites a man and a woman in a unique, wonderful, and unbreakable bond of love.

## Outline and Argument of Song of Songs

The Song of Songs is a dialogue in which Solomon and his best wife ("the Shulammite") express their love for each other early in their marriage. There is also a third party in the dialogue, "the daughters of Jerusalem," which are female attendants of the Shulammite. The entire song was sung on a single occasion, and is a celebration of the couple's married love. However, there appears to be a progression in the book from the initial attraction to deepening affection, including various recollections of the couple's past experiences. The book ends with an epilogue which reflects on love, followed by the departure of the couple to a private place.

The Song of Songs is difficult to understand in English without headings or breaks supplied by translators, because the gender and number of the speakers and addressees are contained in the Hebrew verbs, nouns, and pronouns, but not in their English equivalents. The identification of speakers by a translator's headings might seem arbitrary to the English reader, but the gender and number of the speaker and addressee are usually objectively marked in Hebrew, and such markings are rightly included in a translation. Once changes of speaker are marked, the shape of the dialogue becomes plain, and the book is readily understood.

Since the Song of Songs is a dialogue, the argument and outline are combined below in a dialogue format.

**Heading (1:1):** The heading of the book identifies it as the ultimate song, whose author is Solomon.

**Shulammite (1:2-4a):** The Shulammite expresses her longing and love for Solomon.

**Daughters of Jerusalem (1:4b):** The friends of the bride express their happiness for her.

**Shulammite (1:5-7):** The Shulammite expresses her longing to be taken by Solomon and find rest.

**Daughters of Jerusalem (1:8):** The friends direct the Shulammite towards Solomon's residence.

**Solomon (1:9-10):** Solomon, speaking for the first time, praises his bride's beauty.

**Daughters of Jerusalem (1:11):** The friends respond to Solomon's praise by promising to make ornaments for the bride.

**Shulammite (1:12-14):** The Shulammite describes her husband's sweetness to her.

**Solomon (1:15):** Solomon briefly praises his wife's beauty once again.

**Shulammite (1:16–2:1):** The Shulammite praises Solomon's comeliness, and observes how beautifully husband, wife, and their house fit together.

**Solomon (2:2):** Solomon agrees with his wife's description of herself as a lily, and commends her as standing out above all other women.

**Shulammite (2:3-6):** The Shulammite rejoices in Solomon's possession of her as his wife.

**Shulammite (2:7):** The Shulammite's refrain: do not try to artificially stimulate love.

**Shulammite (2:8-13):** The Shulammite wistfully recalls a visit to the country by the honeymooning couple.

**Solomon (2:14):** Solomon responds to his wife's call by wooing her in turn.

**Shulammite (2:15-17):** The Shulammite revels in the unhindered intimacy of their marriage.

**Shulammite (3:1-4):** The Shulammite recalls an instance when she woke up in the middle of the night and searched the city until she found Solomon.

**Shulammite (3:5):** The Shulammite's refrain: do not try to artificially stimulate love.

**Shulammite (3:6-11):** The Shulammite describes Solomon's royal procession, possibly at the couple's wedding.

**Solomon (4:1-5):** Solomon praises his wife's beauty.

**Solomon (4:6-15):** Solomon expresses his overwhelming desire to enjoy intimacy with his pure, lovely wife.

**Shulammite (4:16):** The Shulammite invites Solomon to enjoy marital intimacy with her.

**Solomon (5:1):** Solomon claims the Shulammite as his own.

**Shulammite (5:2-8):** The Shulammite recalls an instance, perhaps early in the couple's marriage, in which she dreamed that Solomon was looking for her, then awoke to find that he was not there, upon which she went out to look for him.

**Daughters of Jerusalem (5:9):** The daughters ask the Shulammite what is special about her beloved.

**Shulammite (5:10-16):** The Shulammite responds to the prompt by praising Solomon's outstanding comeliness.

**Daughters of Jerusalem (6:1):** The daughters ask the Shulammite where her lover is.

**Shulammite (6:2-3):** The Shulammite responds that her lover is with her.

**Solomon (6:4-9):** In response to the Shulammite's praise of Solomon's unmatched handsomeness, Solomon praises the Shulammite's unmatched beauty.

**Daughters of Jerusalem (6:10):** The daughters respond by agreeing with Solomon's praise of the Shulammite.

**Shulammite (6:11-12):** The Shulammite recalls a reunion with her lover after a brief separation.

**Daughters of Jerusalem (6:13a):** The daughters call for the Shulammite to return to them, so they can admire her beauty.

**Solomon (6:13b):** Solomon compares the gaze of the daughters of Jerusalem upon the Shulammite to the admirers of a graceful dance.

**Solomon (7:1-9a):** Solomon praises his wife's beauty again, moving from the feet up.

**Shulammite (7:9b-13):** The Shulammite calls Solomon to come to her for marital relations.

**Shulammite (8:1-3):** The Shulammite expresses her longing for a constant display of affection for her lover.

**Shulammite (8:4):** The Shulammite's refrain: do not try to artificially stimulate love.

**Daughters of Jerusalem (8:5a):** The daughters observe the married couple's mutual affection.

**Shulammite (8:5b):** The Shulammite recalls her initial union with Solomon.

**Shulammite (8:6-7):** The Shulammite reflects on the unbreakable bond of the couple's love, which was given, not procured.

**Daughters of Jerusalem (8:8-9):** The speakers of 8:8-9 are unclear. This may be a flashback to the Shulammite's youth, in which her brothers promise to find her an excellent husband if she has kept herself pure, but not to give her in marriage if she has played loose.

**Shulammite (8:10-12):** The Shulammite affirms that she has kept herself pure, and, as a result, has found rest with a husband in a home.

**Solomon (8:13):** Solomon asks his wife to call her away for private intimacy.

**Shulammite (8:14):** The song ends with the Shulammite's invitation to Solomon, and the couple's departure.

## Bibliography for Song of Songs

Burrowes, George. *A Commentary on the Song of Solomon*. London: Banner of Truth Trust, 1958.

Carr, G. Lloyd. *The Song of Solomon: An Introduction and Commentary*. Tyndale Old Testament Commentaries. Downers Grove, IL: Inter-Varsity Press, 1984.

Deere, Jack S. "Song of Songs." Pages 1009-25 in *The Bible Knowledge Commentary: Old Testament*, ed. John F. Walvoord and Roy B. Zuck. Colorado Springs: Chariot Victor, 1985.

Delitzsch, Franz. *Commentary on the Song of Songs and Ecclesiastes*. Translated by M. G. Easton. Biblical Commentary on the Old Testament. Reprint: Grand Rapids: Eerdmans, 1950.

Durham, James. *Clavis Cantici: Or, An Exposition of the Song of Solomon*. Aberdeen: George and Robert King, 1840.

Fredericks, Daniel C. and Daniel J. Estes. *Ecclesiastes & the Song of Songs*. Apollos Old Testament Commentary, ed. David W. Baker and Gordon J. Wenham, vol. 16. Downers Grove, IL: InterVarsity Press, 2010.

Garrett, Duane. "Song of Songs." Pages 1-265 in *Song of Songs, Lamentations*. Word Biblical Commentary, vol. 23B. Nashville: Thomas Nelson, 2004.

Gordis, Robert. *The Song of Songs and Lamentations: A Study, Modern Translation and Commentary*. Rev. ed. New York: Ktav, 1974.

Harper, Andrew. *The Song of Solomon: With Introduction and Notes*. Cambridge Bible for Schools and Colleges. Cambridge: Cambridge, 1902.

Hess, Richard S. *Song of Songs*. Baker Commentary on the Old Testament Wisdom and Psalms, ed. Tremper Longman III. Grand Rapids: Baker, 2005.

Hubbard, David A. *Ecclesiastes, Song of Solomon*. Communicator's Commentary, ed. Lloyd J. Ogilvie, vol. 15B. Dallas: Word, 1991.

Keel, Othmar. *The Song of Songs*. Translated by Frederick J. Gaiser. Continental Commentaries. Minneapolis: Fortress Press, 1994.

Kingsbury, T. L. "The Song of Solomon." In *The Holy Bible with an Explanatory and Critical Commentary*, ed. F. C. Cook, vol. 4, 664-702. Cambridge: C. J. Clay, 1892.

Kinlaw, Dennis F. "Song of Songs." Pages 1199-1244 in *The Expositor's Bible Commentary*, vol. 5. Grand Rapids: Zondervan, 1991.

Longman, Tremper, III. *Song of Songs*. New International Commentary on the Old Testament. Grand Rapids: Eerdmans, 2001.

McGee, J. Vernon. "Song of Solomon." In *Thru the Bible with J. Vernon McGee*, vol. 3, 142-82. Nashville: Thomas Nelson, 1982.

Mitchell, Christopher W. *The Song of Songs*. Concordia Commentary. Saint Louis: Concordia, 2003.

Murphy, Roland E. *A Commentary on the Book of Canticles or The Song of Songs*. Edited by S. Dean McBride, Jr. Hermeneia. Minneapolis: Fortress Press, 1990.

Norris, Richard A., Jr., ed. and trans. *The Song of Songs Interpreted by Early Christian and Medieval Commentators*. The Church's Bible, ed. Robert Louis Wilken. Grand Rapids: Eerdmans, 2003.

Pope, Marvin H. *Song of Songs: A New Translation with Introduction and Commentary*. Anchor Bible, vol. 7C. Garden City, NY: Doubleday, 1977.

Provan, Iain. *Ecclesiastes, Song of Songs*. NIV Application Commentary. Grand Rapids: Zondervan, 2001.

Schwab, George M. "Song of Songs." Pages 367-431 in *The Expositor's Bible Commentary: Revised Edition*, vol. 6. Grand Rapids: Zondervan, 2008.

Snaith, John G. *The Song of Songs*. New Century Bible Commentary. Grand Rapids: Eerdmans, 1993.

Wright, J. Robert, and Thomas C. Oden, eds. *Proverbs, Ecclesiastes, Song of Solomon*. Ancient Christian Commentary on Scripture: Old Testament, vol. 9. Downers Grove, IL: InterVarsity Press, 2005.

44162816R00077

Made in the USA
Charleston, SC
16 July 2015